Pagan Generation
A Young Persons Guide to Paganism

by
Luthaneal Adams

Pagan Generation
A Young Persons Guide to Paganism
ISBN 978-1-9079-6313-1

Published by
Hedge Witchery Books
www.hedge-witcherybooks.com

Illustrations
Copyright © Laura Smith 2012

Content
Copyright © Luthaneal Adams 2012

All rights reserved. No part of this publication may be reproduced, stored in a retrieval system, or transmitted in any form or by any means, electronic, mechanical, photocopying, recording or otherwise, without the prior permission of the copyright owner.

Pagan Generation

With Special thanks to:
Andrew Pardy, for lending his keen eye and Heathen mind.
Mike Stygal, for making time and sharing his wisdom.
Laura Smith, for the amazing artwork.

Contents

So, you want to be a Pagan?
Finding the Divine
Walking the Path - Going it alone Vs. Practising with a group
Building a Pagan Practice
A Theory of Magic
Pagan Rituals

Pagan Paths
Wicca: The Old Religion
Druidry: The Spirit of the Land
Religio Romana: The Spirit of Rome
Heathenry: True to the Gods
Celticism: Recovering the Old Ways
Hellenismos: Glory of Olympus
Shamanism: To Walk with the Spirit
Kemeticism: Path of the Black Land
Eclectic Paganism: Ancient Approach, Modern Spirit

Pagan Generation - Know Thyself

So, you want to be a Pagan?

Paganism is quite possibly one the fastest growing religious movements in the world, especially among teenagers. But what exactly does it mean to be "Pagan"? The technical definition of Pagan, simply means "belonging to any non-Abrahamic faith" or to put it another way: any religion that isn't Judaism, Christianity or Islam. However, the word Pagan has come to mean something a lot more specific in the modern day, commonly being associated with things like witchcraft and ancient European religions. These days Pagan is generally used to refer to certain nature based religions and those that attempt to follow the old Gods of the ancient world.

Paganism itself is not a religion, but instead describes a great number of religions that all have different Gods, rituals and beliefs. So how can you find out what path is right for you? This isn't an easy question to answer for a lot of us. The majority of young Pagans will start out alone on their path and literally have the world at their feet. This can be a brilliant time for young Pagans. Your journey is just beginning and you start to feel a spiritual awakening within you. The more you learn the stronger this feeling becomes and at this point in time that feeling is your best guide. This is a time for learning and growth. The best advice that can be given to you now is to learn from as many sources as possible. Read books, search on the internet, join web forums and visit psychic fairs. As you learn, let that feeling inside you be a guide that leads you on your path. If something takes your interest, then stick with it and delve deeper!

Over time you will find your feet firmly on your path and eventually, you may even feel as though the Gods themselves are calling you home.

What Pagan religions are there?

There are a great many Pagan religions in existence today, some older than others, with more being revived as time goes on. Here are some of the most prominent religions that you may encounter in your journey, but this is by no means a complete list of all the Pagan religions out there:

Wicca
Possibly the most well known of the modern Pagan religions and undoubtedly the one that is easiest to find in book stores. Wicca came into being around the 1950's, created by a man named Gerald Gardner. He created Wicca based on the spiritual teachings of many other sources, some old, some new and all from different places. However, Wicca itself did not exist until Gardner brought together all these teachings and combined them into his own religion. Wicca worships a God and Goddess, who symbolically represent the path of human life and the passage of the natural world. The religion also incorporates witchcraft into its beliefs, with the idea of magic being very important for use in rituals, as well as spells.

Wiccans celebrate eight festivals that coincide with the changing seasons. These are the four Sabbats of Samhain (31st October), Imbolc (1st February), Beltane (1st May), Lughnasadh (1st August), and also the two Equinoxes and Solstices of Yule (Winter Solstice, 22nd December), Eostra (Vernal Equinox, 22nd March), Litha (Summer Solstice, 22nd June) and Mabon (Autumn Equinox, 22nd September).

You can find out about Wicca online and in books, as a lot of its teachings have made their way into the public domain. These teachings are known as "Outer Court" Material and can be accessed by anyone expressing an interest in the religion. But Wicca is also a mystery religion, which means that to access the rest (the Inner Court Material) you must be Initiated into a Coven. However, many people are happy to follow a path based on the Outer Court material available to the public.

Druidry
The Druids were religious tribal leaders that can trace their lineage back for thousands of years. But unfortunately, they didn't write anything down, so all we know of their beliefs and practices comes from archaeology and a few histories written by the Romans. As such, modern Druids do not seek to revive this ancient religion, but instead emulate it based on the stories and myths that have survived through the centuries. These myths and legends form a very

important part of modern Druidry, used as teaching aids and keys to spiritual enlightenment.

Druidry doesn't have any particular Gods, but instead its followers are free to honour whatever Gods or spirits they feel are best for them, if any. There are very few fixed beliefs in Druidry; instead modern Druidry is more of a unified philosophy that seeks understanding through stories, divination and communing with the natural world. Druidry is a very holistic religion that sees the natural world as sacred and to be revered. To Druids, all things in nature are equal and deserve respect as pieces of the larger whole. The religion also has a very strong belief in the Spirit World, though each Druid may view it in their own way. They believe that when we die we go to the Spirit World prior to being reborn again, and that we may also come to know the spirit world through trance, meditation and dreams. There are three central goals that druids seek: Creativity, Love and Wisdom.

Heathenry

Heathenry is an attempt to reconstruct the ancient religion of the Germanic people. There are various paths within the broader spectrum of Heathenry, including Odinism and Asatru.

The Asatruar (followers of Asatru) worship the ancestral Gods of the Germanic people, usually with a particular focus upon the Icelandic expression of that religion. You have probably heard of many of their Gods, such as Odin, Thor and Loki. Heathenry is a polytheistic religion, which means it believes in many Gods whom it views as all being separate and unique entities. However, Heathens also commonly believe in other beings such as spirits of nature and ancestor spirits.

The main belief of Asatru is that the Gods can and do interact with mortals and that through ritual and devotion people can form a relationship with the Gods. The height of Asatru beliefs rest around the concepts of fairness and honour, disallowing the discrimination of anyone based on race, gender, age, nationality, etc. Family and community are also very important in Asatru and each person is expected to act well and live up to their responsibilities. There are Nine Noble Virtues in Asatru: Courage, Truth, Honor, Fidelity, Discipline, Hospitality, Industriousness, Self-Reliance and Perseverance. Asatru also make use of magic, most often through the use of Runes.

Hellenism

Another polytheistic religion, Hellenism seeks to reconstruct the religious practices of the ancient Greeks. Hellenists believe in the Greek Gods, such as

Zeus, Athena and Dionysus, whom they worship by making offerings and prayers in exchange for the blessings of the Gods. Many Hellenists also enact the festivals that were celebrated by the classical Greeks. Hellenism has a lot of benefits in its attempts to reconstruct these ancient practices because they were so well recorded. Scholars have uncovered a lot of details about the religious practices of these people and followers can also draw on literary sources such as Homer and Hesiod.

Hellenism has several large organisations, including the Supreme Council of Ethnikoi Hellenes, who hold large festivals for followers of the religion and are petitioning to gain access to worship in the traditional temple sites of the faith.

Celtic Reconstruction
A new religion based on old ideas. Celtic Reconstructionism uses surviving information from folklore and mythology to recreate the various religious practices of the Celtic people. The Celts cover a wide variety of European people, who share similar yet unique cultures. Each has their own Gods, practices and beliefs, but there is very often an overlap in certain concepts. Celtic beliefs hail from the ancient religions of Britain, Ireland and Gaul (European continent). Most Celtic people tend to have a variety of Gods, a reverence for the spirits of Ancestors and a belief in the existence of other spiritual beings associated with certain places or things, such as the spirits of rivers or Guardian spirits to certain sacred places. Many Celtic people believe in reincarnation, though some also believe in specific afterlife realms where followers of the Gods may go to when they die.

Many Celtic Reconstructionists celebrate seasonal festivals in a similar style to Wicca, but some also have unique rituals based on the specific Gods that they follow. Some common Celtic deities are The Dagda, who is the supreme defender of the Tribe, Lugh the Irish multi-skilled hero-God, Danu the mother Goddess, Cernunnos the horned God, and Abnoba the Goddess of forests and rivers.

Kemeticism
Kemeticism is a revivalist religion that attempts to bring to life the traditional religious ways of ancient Egypt. Kemetics follow the Egyptian Gods, whom they view like parents that can guide us in our lives. While many see these Gods as individual deities, many Kemetics view each God as a manifestation of the greater divine power of the universe. One of the most important beliefs in Kemeticism is the existence of Ma'at. Ma'at is seen as the natural way of creation. It is a force of balance that maintains the workings of the universe and keeps them running smoothly. It is a state of order within nature and society that must be maintained through righteous law, justice and truth.

Followers of Kemeticism attempt to uphold the ideals of the Declaration of Innocence, which is an ancient text that lists all the things a soul should be innocent of when they come into the afterlife. Mortals that have been deemed worthy in the afterlife go on to reside in Duat, the land of the dead. Some Kemetics also believe that humans have the option to reincarnate, also.

Kemeticism potentially has the most celebrations out of all the Pagan religions, almost all of which are unique to this religion. There are several festivals per month, with some months having almost one a day; however it is usually left up to the individual to decide which festivals are relevant to them.

Eclectic Paganism

Of course, you don't need to follow any one religion to be Pagan. In fact, a great number of Pagans choose not to. These Pagans either possess their own beliefs that are utterly unique to them, or create their own path by taking different things from several religions and combining them together in a way that suites them best. This is known as Eclectic Paganism.

A lot of people find this the easier road to travel, as it is completely free-form, giving you the power to sculpt your faith into something that truly represents what you believe. Of course this also has the potential downside that you're pretty much destined to remain solitary in your practices, so it can be a rather lonely path. However, that doesn't mean that you won't find people who share your beliefs. Paganism attracts an extremely diverse group and you will always be able to find people that are open to your beliefs and just as willing to share their own. Just check a few Pagan forums on the internet and I am sure you will make a few friends.

So many choices, what do I choose?

Right now, don't worry about it too much. You have all the time in the world to refine your beliefs and find the niche that suits you best, so don't worry too much about slapping a label on yourself. Now isn't really the time to be overly concerned with that. No, now is the time for you to try and get a better understanding of what you actually believe. If any of the religions mentioned appeal to you at all, then do some research on them. Trust your gut. You are the best judge to your own spirituality.

The most important thing to remember when taking your first steps into Paganism is that there is no right or wrong path. There is just the path that is right for you and that is all you really need to concern yourself with. Remember, your first step on the path begins within you. Your Pagan journey is an internal one. It is a spiritual process by which you come to learn who you are and who you want to be. It is about understanding the world around you and coming to know your position in it. Finally it is about connecting to something that is greater than you are and opening a door to allow that into your life so that you might become greater too.

But here is the really good news

Becoming a Pagan has never been easier! We are living in a Pagan revolution and more people are turning to this path every day. Paganism is more accessible and approachable than it has been in a very long time. The shops are loaded with books and materials, meaning that not only can you get your hands on some good information, but you can also easily buy the tools of the trade. Also, it is pretty easy to find shops and stalls that specifically sell Pagan and witchcraft related goods. So whether you are looking for Tarot Cards, Runes, candles or a new chalice, you are sure to find somewhere that can accommodate you and chances are that it wont be very far away.

Most Pagan and New-Age shops will also be run by people who are more than willing to talk to you about it all and recommend some good resources. However, try not to let any one person's opinion be too influential, after all this is your path and not theirs. Indeed, that goes for books and websites too. When you find something you are interested in, don't just stop there; keep digging deeper to discover more about it. No one source holds all the pieces and in this Pagan revolution there so many places to look.

Here is the not-so-good news

Yes, there are a lot of sources out there. But are they all good? Certainly not. Although there is a vast array of books and websites about Paganism, not all of them are as accurate as we might hope. Some are even down right wrong. That isn't to say that any spiritual path is necessarily worse than any other, but it does mean that sometimes people get their facts wrong. For this reason, it is probably best to take everything with a pinch of salt until you know for sure whether it is true or not. That being said, I can provide you with a little help in that area by dispelling a few myths that you may run into in your journey:

The Burning Times

Some authors like the talk about the "Burning Times". The Burning Times is a mythical time when thousands (some say millions) of witches were burned at the stake. While it is true that witchcraft was illegal for a very long time, very few people were burned for witchcraft. The punishment for witchcraft was most often hanging and the majority of those killed were really Christians who had been falsely accused. Of course, it was wrong to make witchcraft illegal in the first place, but lets not disrespect the memories of those who suffered by making it into something it wasn't.

I'm a witch, that makes me a Wiccan

The easiest way to put this is as so: Every Wiccan is a witch, but not every witch is a Wiccan. Wicca and witchcraft aren't the same things. Wicca is a religion that uses witchcraft, but there are other religions and paths that also use witchcraft. Witchcraft itself is not a religion; it is exactly what it says it is: a craft.

Wicca is older than dirt

Some authors like to foster the idea that Wicca is many thousands or millions of years old, perhaps even as old as humanity itself. This is not the case. Although some aspects of Wicca date back quite far, Wicca itself is less than 100 years old. Simply because some bits come from older sources, that doesn't make them Wicca. As a Wiccan once said to me, "Flour isn't the same as a cake."

Pagans and Wiccans and witches, oh my!

These words are not interchangeable. Not all Pagans are Wiccan. Not all witches are Wiccan. Not all witches are Pagan. Any author who can't make this simple distinction isn't likely to get much else right.

Pagans believe…

I'm not sure there is any accurate way to finish this sentence. Paganism is a collection of many different beliefs and there is no one belief that is held by all Pagans.

Religion X is keeping us down!
There are authors out there who have a real persecution complex. They seem to blame all the woes of the world on a certain religion. Sometimes this is a historical view (like the Burning Times mentioned already), other times it is an insistence that certain groups in the modern day are trying to destroy their religion. Often Christianity comes under this kind of fire, but these authors are just as willing to take pot-shots at other Pagans. In short, these people have their own agenda. Don't let their bias towards others affect the way that you approach other religions.

Think of these myths as warning signs that can help you to identify how good a source really is. Any book, website or person that is saying things like these probably doesn't know as much as they think they do. Still, we are all learning, right?

But it's not all bad news. In amongst it all there is some really good information from some really good authors. I won't recommend any here, as all authors write on their own subjects and those areas may not be right for you. As starting Pagans, it is important to find your own way.

But some recommendations would have been useful
Oh okay, you twisted my arm. But don't feel obliged to agree with these authors simply because they have been recommended in this book. Remember, make up your own minds and follow what feels right to you.

Some useful websites
The Cauldron: http://www.ecauldron.com/index.php
A general Pagan site that carries some good articles about the different Pagan religions.

Some Good books
The Witches' Bible by Janet Farrar and Stewart Farrar
This book provides you with everything you need to know to practice witchcraft in the Wiccan style.

Pagan Paths: A Guide to Wicca, Druidry, Asatru, Shamanism and Other Pagan Practices by Pete Jennings

A definitive introduction to the Pagan spiritual paths that anyone new to Paganism can easily read.

The Book of Druidry by Ross Nichols
This is the primary book on Druidry, giving information about all the significant beliefs and practices.

The Neteru of Kemet: An Introduction by Tamara Siuda-Legan
A good book for people who want a beginners look at Kemeticism.

Recommended Groups

The Pagan Federation: http://www.paganfed.org/
Produces a regular magazine for members and is an excellent way to network with other Pagans.

Children of Artemis: http://www.witchcraft.org/
A very accessible group with forums and articles. Members also gain discounts at Witchfest.

Events and Networking*

The Pagan Federation: http://www.paganfed.org/
Very good for networking and finding local groups in your area. Check your district on their site for contact details.
For those outside of Great Britain, try The Pagan Federation International (http://www.paganfederation.org/) for the same kind of help in other countries.

Witchfest
Witchfest is the world's largest witchcraft festival and is held throughout the year across Britain. The event offers seminars, stalls, live music and the opportunity to meet a lot of other Pagans.

Witchvox: http://www.witchvox.com/
Here you can find a registry of many different Pagan groups in different countries, as well as ways to contact them.

Safety!!!
- If you are trying to meet people and find groups make sure that you have spoken with them in length before you try to organize a meeting.
- When meeting someone for the first time, be careful! If you are under 18 tell your parents who you are meeting and where, then make sure you

have an adult with you. If you are over 18, play it safe anyway, let friends or family know where you will be and who you will be with.
- All ways meet in a public place.
- If the person you are meeting makes you uncomfortable, excuse yourself and leave.
- Do not do anything that you don't want to do. It doesn't matter what the other person says, if you don't feel comfortable with it, then it isn't right for you.

Your journey begins...

Now you have absolutely everything you could ever need to begin your journey into Paganism. This isn't supposed to be some kind of ultimate guide to the Pagan world, but it is a doorway into it. Now it is up to you to walk through and discover the path that is right for you.

May your Gods find you safely...

Sweet dreams.

Finding the Divine

One of the hardest (and also perhaps, easiest) questions that a Pagan can face, concerns their relationship with the divine and how they perceive it.

"Which Gods are right for me?" Is essentially the forwarding question and it can be more complex than you may think. This question looks at the idea of not only the many different Gods available, but also how you relate to them. In turn this becomes an examination of yourself.

Views of Divinity

The first step in finding the God or Gods that are right for you is putting some thought into how you generally perceive the divine. Look deep inside yourself and ask "what does Deity really mean to me?" This may seem like a simple question at first, but once you engage in some self-exploration, you may find that the answer is a lot deeper than you had first imagined.

Here in the West, we are very often presented with a pre-established idea of "God" and what that is. Predominantly this is in a Judeo-Christian sense, but things are considerably different in Paganism. Pagans have a vast array of perceptions of the divine, some you may be aware of and some you may not. But even if we examine the already known ideas of the Christian God, it can give us pause for thought, despite the familiar territory. It is a being of spiritual presence, human presence and Godly presence. One being taking a role in three worlds. Even considering the meaning of this can leave us grasping for understand, but this triune God idea is not too uncommon. We see it present in religions like Hinduism, Irish Celticism and perhaps more familiarly to you in the form of the Wiccan Goddess, who is presented as Maiden, Mother and Crone.

There are a great many ways to look at the divine and it can take some soul-searching to really get to the heart of your beliefs on the matter and even when you do, you may find that they change over time. Some of you will probably be coming to this book already with an idea of what you believe – or at the very least, what you *don't* believe. So what is offered here is an opportunity to really come to understand those beliefs and then find a way to embody them and interact with them in all your workings. For this we will begin slowly, by looking at different forms in which the divine may exist:

Monotheism

Some Pagans are monotheistic. This means that they believe that there is just one single God, possessing a single personality, even though that personality may manifest in different ways. Although you may be more familiar with this in regards to religions like Christianity, there are some Pagans who hold this perception of the divine.

Polytheism

This is the belief in many Gods, all with different personalities and characteristics. This is a belief that you will probably encounter quite a lot in Paganism. The ancient Greeks, Romans, Egyptians, Celts and Heathens (to name but a few), held this belief and so you will find it is quite prevalent these days with people who seek to recreate these religions. In this belief, each God is unique and as much their own person as we humans are. To some the Gods are higher beings, separate from humanity, while to others even humans can attain Godhood. Polytheism covers a very large spectrum of beliefs, but all have one thing in common: the belief in multiple Gods.

Duotheism

This is a very particular form of polytheism, focusing on the belief in just two deities. Wicca is one such religion, with a God and Goddess, who in this case represent the masculine and feminine, while simultaneously embodying the cycles of the natural world. This isn't true of all duotheisms though. The classification of a duo-religion is the following of just two Gods, whatever their relationship may be to each other.

Monolatry

Some people also believe that all Gods and Goddesses are equally valid, as they are all expressions of one singular deity or source. This, in a way, is a very unique form of religion, often combining monotheism and polytheism to a degree. The best example of this is Kemeticism, which has a very large variety of Gods, but many of it's followers (though by no means all) see them all as different aspects of an ultimately unknowable, self-created Oneness. This point of view or one similar to it, has become very popular in modern Paganism, especially among more eclectic paths.

There are many views that touch on this idea or concepts that are very similar to it, such as Pantheism, Panentheism and in some ways, monism. However, dividing up the differences between these three could take more space than is available here. So, I would suggest that if this is your view of the divine, you may find it interesting to do some additional research into these things.

Atheism

It might seem like a strange one to add to the list, but truth be told, atheism is a perfectly valid view of the divine when it comes to Paganism. Atheism is the disbelief in any kind of God. Granted, this isn't going to be an obvious choice for someone seeking a connection to the divine, however it is perfectly possible to find the occasional atheist among the casual herds of modern Paganism. Most of the time this tends to apply to witches who have no belief in Gods or Goddesses. Again, it's rare, but it does happen.

Agnosticism
Essentially the belief that you can never really know if there are any Gods. However, being as the direct purpose of this article is to help you determine just that, I'll not bother going any further on this one. But if by the end of your search, you are still unsure what you believe about Deity, then this is a perfectly acceptable label to take if you wish. Once you have decided your basic view of the divine, then it may help you forge a better relationship with it/them by coming to identify them in the way that feels right for you.

If you are a polytheist, for example, then one of the following pantheons may strike a personal chord with you, however, if you are more of an all-in-one kind of person then you may simply be given to find the Gods that you feel the best connection to in order to forge a relationship with the greater divine essence. At this stage, only you can know what feels right.

But look at the following brief descriptions and see if anything there sparks your interest. If it does, then begin some research on those things. If you can, talk to people who follow that path and don't be afraid to ask questions. Remember, questioning is the best way to understanding.

Who are the Gods?

There are a great many Gods and Goddesses out there, spanning a wide range of different Pagan religions and beliefs. From the Aesir to the Wiccan Lord and Lady, a new Pagan can seem spoilt for choice. But they are all very different and most likely you wont want to form a close personal relationship with them all. Because that is what you are essentially doing, coming to the Gods and forming a relationship, but one unlike any other you have known.

But what Gods are there, exactly? Well, given the sheer number of them, it would take at least a small book to list them all, so instead here is a brief summary of the more well known pantheons of Gods:

The Aesir

The Aesir are the principle Gods of Norse mythology, ruled by the All-Father, Odin. As well as the Aesir, there is also a second group of Gods known as the Vanir, who were at one time at war with the Aesir. However, these two groups were eventually assimilated into each other after forming a peace treaty. The most well known Gods of the Aesir are probably:

> ***Odin***: the chief God often seen as very wise and powerful.
> ***Thor:*** the God of thunder, seen as a strong and noble warrior.
> ***Freya:*** Goddess of female power, seen to be beautiful and also associated with magic and death.
> ***Tyr:*** God of justice, who sacrificed his own hand in order to shackle the great wolf Fenrir.
> ***Baldr:*** a God of rebirth and innocence, who it is said will be reborn after all the Gods have died.

However, following the Norse deities needn't be restricted to the ranks of the Aesir. Followers of Heathenry may also call upon the power and wisdom of their ancestor spirits and other beings of the natural and supernatural world.

The Netjer and Neteret

These are the terms used by the ancient Egyptians to refer to their Gods and Goddesses, Netjer being the word for God and Neteret being the word for Goddess. The Gods of the ancient Egyptians span a great a varied mythology that was recorded in great detail by the Egyptians. The chief among the Gods is ***Ra***, who is famed for pulling the sun across the sky in a golden chariot. Other popular deities in this pantheon are:

Anubis: the Jackal-headed God who assists in the judging of the dead and guides the worthy to the throne of Osiris.
Osiris: Osiris is the lord of the underworld, but also symbolises the regenerative powers of nature.
Isis: a mother Goddess who is the sister and consort to Osiris, known for her magical powers, especially concerning life and death. She is also seen as a great ruler and is the mother of Horus.
Horus: a heroic God who is the son of Isis and Osiris. He is famed for avenging the death of his father at the hands of the God *Seth*. He became a great ruler of Egypt and was revered as a sky God, with the sun and moon visible in his eyes.
Hathor: the Goddess of joy, love, dance and song. She cares for mothers and children, but also nurtured the dead on their way to the underworld.
Bast: or Bastet, is a benevolent Goddess, depicted with a cat's head. She was a fertility Goddess, but also protected humanity from disease and evil spirits.

Many of the Egyptian Gods are combined at different times in Egyptian history, as their concepts merge with each other, while some Gods are formed as aspects of other Gods. For example Bastet (to some) is formed of the benevolent side of Sekhmet, while Sekhmet was brought into being when Ra transformed Hathor into his avenger for a time. Meanwhile Horus, as a God of the Sky, was sometimes worshiped as "Horus of the Horizon" and seen as a sun God. In this aspect he was eventually associated with Ra, becoming Ra-Herakhty.

The Olympians

The Greek Gods were mythically said to reside upon Mount Olympus and hence are sometimes known as the Olympian Gods. Their mythology is very deep and detailed, coming from a great culture of myth-makers and storytellers, where these stories where often seen as moral lessons, designed to entertain the listener while teaching a lesson. The stories of the Gods were seen in a similar light, often taken with a pinch of salt, as they all at once believed in the Gods, but also knew the purpose of their myths. Amongst the Olympian Gods were:

Zeus: the chief of the Gods, who could wield the power of the lightening bolt.
Hera: a mother Goddess and the wife of Zeus. She is a Goddess of marriage and her myths are often tales of how she punishes those women who have affairs with her husband.
Ares: was the God of war. He is a mighty warrior and a passionate lover.

Artemis: the virgin huntress. She is a Goddess of the wild, natural places.
Hades: the ruler of the underworld. He resides over the realm of the dead.
Persephone: a Goddess of life and death as represented through the cycle of the seasons. She spends half the year in the underworld with Hades and half the year with her mother, **Demeter**, who restores the Earth to life upon her return.
Aphrodite: the Goddess of love in all its forms. She is seen as a beautiful woman and associated with beauty and fertility.

Following the Greek Gods is a matter of all at once acknowledging their existence, while also paying heed to what they represent and the lessons conveyed in their stories, particularly how a person must accept responsibility for who they are and their place within society.

The Tuatha De Danann

In their time, the Celtic people were spread widely across Europe and the British Isles and over that vast distance they could be found to worship a great many Gods. But amongst the Celts of Ireland, the most popular Gods were known as the Tuatha De Danann. This translated as "the people of the Goddess Danu", who were the last generation of Gods to rule over Ireland. These Gods were very wise and highly skilled in magic. The Tuatha De Danann appear to be known to most Celtic people of the time, as their names can be found in Welsh mythology and on inscriptions on the European continent. The main Gods of the Tuatha De Danann were:

Danu: the founder and mother of the Tuatha De Danann.
Dagda: Dagda is a God of life and death. He is seen as a great warrior and a great magician.
Morrigan: She is a Goddess of war and battle. She takes many forms, including that of a crow or as three hags, or with her other Goddess aspects known as **Babd** and **Macha**.
Brigid: Brigid is a triple-Goddess of fire, embodied in her aspects as Fire of Inspiration, Fire of the Hearth and Fire of the Forge. In these aspects she is associated with the arts, the home & childbirth, and craftsmanship. Her festival is Imbolc, held on February 1st.
Lugh: The God of all-skills. This God of the Sun is a fierce warrior and is attributed as joining the ranks of the Tuatha De Danann because he possessed great skill in all fields of excellence, being a warrior, a sorcerer, a craftsman, a scholar, a poet and musician. His traditional feast is Lughnasadh on August 1st.

Eventually, according to their mythology, the Tuatha De Danann retired from their ruling position, taking residence beneath the Earth, where they came to be known as Aes Sidhe, which became synonymous with faeries over the centuries.

The Lord and Lady
In the Wiccan religion, which is much more recent than any of the previously mentioned religions, there is no traditional mythology. Instead, Wiccans venerate a dualism in the form of the Lord and Lady (also known as the God and Goddess). These two deities embody different identities that change over the course of the year, corresponding to the cycle of the natural world. In place of mythology, Wicca has a kind of seasonal play that takes places upon the stage of the natural world, with its God and Goddess taking the leading role and playing every part. In this way, a story (or perhaps a set of stories) is told in a similar fashion to mythology, but instead of a written or spoken story, it is acted out in the change of the seasons and through the rituals of the religion.

Depending upon who you talk to, the Lord and Lady will sometimes be depicted with different names or in the guises of the Gods and Goddesses of other Pagan religions. However, despite this, one common factor of Wicca is that the real names of their deities are only revealed to people once they have initiated into the religion, where it remains a secret. For these reasons, these deities will simply be termed as the "God" and "Goddess" here:

The Goddess: Wicca has a triune Goddess, meaning that she is viewed in three guises. These are the Maiden, Mother and Crone, who represent the three stages of a woman's life. She is a moon Goddess and with the God, helps symbolise the passage of life, death and rebirth. She is the "all-mother" bringing forth life in the natural world, but also giving birth to the God, whom will later become her lover.

The God: Sometimes referred to a "The Horned God", he is the symbol of masculine power and virility. He embodies the male polarity of nature and humanity, but is also the representation of man's passage of life and death. He is a hunter, who takes life for the good of others, but also a sacrificial king who gives up his life to nourish the natural world and continue into the land of the dead, where he rules.

The Purpose of Mythology

When looking at beings such as the Pagan Gods, it is sometimes hard to take them seriously when you look at their Dungeons & Dragons style mythologies (though lets not forget you would have no Dungeons & Dragons without such colourful real-world mythologies). And it can be difficult to relate to them when they have this fantastical backdrop to them. Well, there are essentially two ways to approach this: The literal and the figurative. You could, if you were so inclined, choose to see these stories as real tales of things that supposedly happened, both in our world and in the mysterious heavens beyond. If this is what you believe then that's up to you, although I will say that you would probably have trouble believing in Ra pulling the sun across the sky when we know today that the sun is stationary. But again, your beliefs have to be your own. Perhaps you will pick and choose, finding that some of these tales may be true and some may not. But if you want to get the fullest understanding of the Gods and their mythologies, then you need to understand the role their tales played in the societies they came from.

Mythology, for a large part, is about telling stories and explaining the world. When our ancestors looked at the workings of the world, they were undoubtedly given to ask (as we still do) "why does that happen?" "What makes that work?" To answer these questions they often produced tales and myths that attempted to explain these things or in some way embody the ideas that they had about how the world works. Sometimes this meant that they believed these myths in a literal sense, at other times it was a way to convey personal theories or deeply held mystical understandings regarding the universe.

It's for this reason that we can't just discount mythology off hand. Through mythology we have the keys to understanding the mystic knowledge of our ancestors, the secrets they knew about our world and the next world, as well as the answers to questions that humanity is still asking today.

What do the Gods tell us in their stories? What lessons do they teach us about ourselves and society? Mythology is a collection of morality and mysticism. Through mythology the Gods show us ways to live and behaviour to idealise. Can we all be as brave as Achilles? As wise as Isis? As noble as Tyr?

We have always had our mythologies to give us these kinds of examples of greatness. Today, our myths are told in comic books and movies. Our popular icons are superheroes and action-movie stars. But is that all mythology is? Are we to assume that the Gods are nothing more than imagined characters in a creative story? Oh no, not even slightly. Myth and legend is about telling stories about things that are real. Did Theseus really slay the Minotaur? Probably not. But Theseus is us, he is the hero that we all could be and the real hero in society. The Minotaur probably wasn't a real beast, but what he represented certainly was. It is similar with the Gods. Mankind is inspired to tell tales of the things he knows, the things he fears and the things he loves. The tales of the Gods are in essence, inspired by the Gods themselves. They are written to celebrate the very real relationships that the Gods have in our lives and to bring focus upon the things that the Gods teach us through those relationships.

We come to understand the Gods and who they are and we express that understanding through myths, which we use to teach others about the lessons that the Gods have to offer us. It is a delicate balance between real events, creative storytelling and the subtle revelation of spiritual truth. As we cut our way between these different aspects of myth and legend, we bring ourselves to the heart of their being: the truth of deity.

The myths relay to us who the Gods are, what they like, the traits they admire and the things that we should strive for in order to reach them. These stories help us to live together and to live well, both among humanity and among the Gods as well.

Aligning yourself to the Gods

I've heard it said time and time again by just about every Pagan I have ever met, that when they found the right path for them, they "just knew". Something inside them clicked immediately and they knew that they had come across something very special. Chances are that it will be the same for you when you find your path – assuming you haven't already.

In a way, that is the beautiful thing about Paganism. It very much relies on you to find your own way and come to understand your own spirituality. I've heard it said that finding the right path is like "coming home" and really that is exactly what it is like. It's a home-calling. You are discovering your place in the world and your very spirit becomes uplifted and seems to ignite with a new found vitality.

But on the flip-side, there are those who say that they didn't choose their path, their path chose them. They may have felt the same 'click', but they also seemed to gain some other kind of recognition, as if the Gods themselves took a direct hand in bringing them onto their path.

One Heathen I spoke to, told me of how he discovered Heathenry and then over the following week several of the Norse Gods came to him in dreams. I know others who have felt similarly about the Lord and Lady in Wicca, feeling as if an intrinsic connection to the natural world sparked within them, as if the God and Goddess were suddenly making themselves known. In Kemeticism, the selection of the Gods plays a vital and official role, where a big part of initiations is the discovery of what God claims you as their own.

But whether you choose the Gods or they choose you, either way it is a magical feeling of recognition and one that could very well change you forever. Once you know which God, Goddess or Gods are the ones for you, you can set about forging and strengthening you connection to them. A good way to mark the beginning of this relationship is through a Dedication Ritual, in which you come before you Gods and announce your loyalty to them. For a guide of how to design your own Dedication Ritual, turn to page 42.

Dedication Rituals such as these are great ways to mark the beginning of your relationship with your new found deities, but that is by no means the end of it. Your relationship to them, like any relationship, should be progressive. You wouldn't see your boyfriend once and then never see him again, nor would you invite the Gods into your life so intimately and then fail to acknowledge them afterwards. Your Gods will undoubtedly be keeping a close eye on you and it will be up to you to make good on your commitment to your path.

Read
Chances are that you haven't just plucked your deity out of the air. So that means that a large amount of people out there have gone before you and left behind a wealth of information on the Gods you are following. To improve your understanding of your Gods, let these people teach you how they have come to know the Gods by reading books on the subject. There are lots of good authors out there, head down to your local library or book store and see what you can find. Or if you have the means, look up authors online and grab some good books from Amazon. You may even be able to find some cheap books on Ebay if you are lucky.

Even if you have a more general idea of deity, rather than a specific God, Goddess or pantheon, you will still find a great wealth of information available out there to give you insights on the divine and how it relates to you. Chances are that *someone* out there is walking a similar path as you and has something to say about it.

Rituals

If you have chosen an established deity, there are probably already certain rituals and holidays associated with them. Learn about these rituals and partake in them when you feel comfortable doing so. But more than this, find out all you can about these things. You will find that a God's rituals and holidays are great insight into the God themselves. Rituals are laced with all manner of symbolism and meaning that teaches you something about the deities and their relationship with us.

Of course, after that the best way to learn is through doing. There is no point in doing a ritual you don't understand, it would just be a chore of meaningless actions to you and that would be dishonourable to your deities and is in no way beneficial to you. But once you do understand the significance of a ritual observation, then by all means, get out there and do it! It is one thing to read about a ritual and understand what it means, but it is something else altogether to be a part of that ritual and understand it from the inside. Don't be a spectator in your religion, take part in the magic!

Living your Life

I doubt that your new God or Goddess will want an automaton for a follower, so take your life and live it well. Likelihood is that the reason your Gods accepted you is because you already display the qualities that they find desirable. So don't just drop your life in lieu or your new found path, instead live your life as part of that path. It is very likely that taking these steps on your spiritual journey will change you greatly, if not immediately, then over time. You may even feel a change within yourself already. But try to keep in mind that your spiritual rebirth doesn't take you away from this world and doesn't remove the friends, family and work that you already have.

But this is a very significant thing in your relationship to your deity. They are also a part of your life now and if you allow them, they will be a beneficial influence to you, giving you a new outlook, an inner strength and a kind of personal guidance that is utterly unique to you. With this you can take the life you have and use the guidance and strength of your Gods to make it the best that you can.

Nobody likes a whiner

As has just been mentioned, you still have your life to live. This means that you also still have all the problems and challenges of day to day life, as well. Finding a connection to the divine isn't an excuse to avoid the bad things in life. The Gods aren't there to solve all your problems for you and you cant magic your way out of everything that you'd rather not do.

Life is for living: good and bad.

The Gods help us to live; they don't do all the work for us. So don't go making rituals petitioning the Gods for every little thing and don't waste your time doing spells to try and avoid all the negative things in life. The Gods are well aware of when you really need them and when you don't, and magic isn't an answer to all your problems. Have some respect for the position the Gods hold and have some faith in your own ability to deal with things.

Honour your Gods
Quite simply, be respectful. We are talking about the divine manifest in nature, and however you view that, it deserves some respect. Personally, I like to think that the Gods have a sense of humour and a good few times I've had a rather amusing chat about the "Horny God", but you and I should both know the difference between having fun and being offensive. I say that if you cant laugh at yourself, then you are taking life too seriously, but at the end of the day there is still a certain degree of appropriateness when dealing with anyone, God or otherwise. You wouldn't (I hope) just insult people without good reason and so don't act in a way that demeans your relationship with your Gods.

You don't need to convert people, talk about your Gods to everyone you meet and advertise your spirituality. Of course, be proud of who you are and what you believe, but there is a time and place for all things, so give the Gods theirs.

Another key way to honour your relationship with the Gods is to make sure that you do what you vow to do. If you make a promise to your Gods, keep it. This includes the vows you made at your Dedication/Initiation (if you've had one) and any that may have followed since.

Another part of honouring your Gods comes in your relationship to other religions. Don't go giving a bad reputation to your religion and your Gods by acting as a negative example. Finding your own Gods and being proud of them isn't an excuse to tear into other religions. You wouldn't like your religion and Gods being disrespected, so show the same courtesy to other people. Even if you encounter people who insult you and your religion, feel free to stick up for yourself, but just be aware of who you are targeting. Just because they may be acting like offensive trolls doesn't mean that is necessarily a reflection on the God they follow and it certainly isn't a reflection on all followers of that religion. Just because another person may be a poor representative of their Gods, doesn't mean that you have to sink to that level and dishonour both yourself and your Gods.

Respect your contemporaries

You most likely aren't the only person following your deity and it's entirely likely that other people may have a few views of the Gods that are different to yours. This in itself doesn't make them wrong. Each person forges their own relationship with the divine that is unique to them and so it may bring to them certain perceptions and insights that it hasn't to you. Likewise, you have a unique relationship with your deity and probably have insights of your own.

But don't get me wrong though, people are certainly free to hold their own views, but that doesn't mean you should just roll over when you really do disagree with something. If you feel someone has a completely unrealistic view of your Gods or religion, then it's your choice if you wish to say so. Just keep in mind that just because you disagree with them, doesn't mean that they will listen. Best you can do is to try to educate them as to your view. If they won't accept it, then there is nothing much you can do. However, don't go thinking that you will always be right. Indeed, prepare for the odd education yourself.

Keep in mind what your Gods want

You came to your Gods for a reason. They/he/she/it probably stood for something that you agree with and from there you have entered a relationship with them. As part and parcel of that package it's probably true that your Gods consider certain qualities to be desirable virtues in their followers. In bringing the Gods into your life and dedicating yourself to them you have made an arrangement. They are in your camp and in return you need to be in theirs. If they commend certain virtues then you probably owe it to them to try and embody those in return for their presence and help in your life. After all, the Gods aren't really going to want to associate with someone who is in opposition to the things they stand for. Chances are that if you have felt called to these Gods, then you probably already have those qualities in abundance, but perhaps now is the time to try and develop those qualities within yourself as part of your commitment to your deities.

A relationship goes both ways

You're following your Gods, whoever they may be and they may make certain demands of character and expect you to behave in a certain way. But let's be realistic here. This isn't a one-way street. Just as you are giving something, so too are the Gods. Or at least we would hope so. Perhaps you should ask yourself "what exactly is it that I want to get out of this relationship?" That isn't a bad question to ask in any kind of relationship, whether it's divine, romantic or a business arrangement. But keep in mind; just like with any kind of relationship, you won't necessarily get everything you want. The desires of both sides have to be reasonable. So think about what it is you desire and whether it is a reasonable to want these things. Then consider what the Gods are offering you and whether you are living up to your side of the commitment.

Don't get above yourself though. Keep in mind that the Gods have a pretty good insight to things and so what you want may not always be necessarily the best thing for them to offer you. This could be an opportunity for you to really think about the difference between the things that you want and the things that you need. Ultimately, I would say that it is up to us to attain the things we want, while the universe has a nice way of providing a path to our fundamental needs. Somewhere in the middle the Gods meet us, giving us the occasional helping hand to what we want and opening new paths to the things we may not even know we need, providing a way to our spiritual well-being and growth.

But every relationship is unique and will depend on how you see your deity and how you are seen in return. It is by no means all about personal gain. What you put into a relationship is proportionate to what you get out of it and the most worthwhile things to put in are love, respect and happiness. We aren't talking about some kind of legal contract here, we are talking about forming a very real connection to the divine and the only way to do that is with an open heart and an open mind. You have to let them in to your life and they will let you into theirs. When you practice your rituals and festivals, you aren't just honouring your Gods, you are celebrating with them. Take joy in your relationship with them and allow them to take joy in their relationship with you.

Pagan Generation

Walking the Path

- Going it alone Vs. Practising with a group -

Once a young Pagan or witch has established what they believe and the path that they wish to follow, they will sooner or later be presented with the choice of walking that path alone or joining a group with similar beliefs. Both methods have advantages and disadvantages that should be considered when deciding whether or not to join others. Are their goals the same as yours? Do they allow you to adequately explore your new beliefs? What do you have to do in order to join? These and many other questions will need to be answered while you determine whether you are better suited to solitary practice or group practice.

Standing before the Gods

The first thing that you should determine about any potential group is whether or not their beliefs are compatible with your own. If the answer is no, then they obviously aren't right for you. Talk to members of the group and find out what they believe to see if they see things in the same way that you do and more importantly, whether or not they will allow you to express your beliefs in a way that you feel is right for you.

Each group will have their own way of practising, whether they are more of a religious group or just a coven of witches following a magical path. This means that they will undoubtedly have certain rituals and practices that they use to express their beliefs and honour any Gods that they may have. Find out as much as you can about these practices to see if you would be comfortable doing them and if you feel that they are a good way for you to come to your Gods. A person's relationship with their deities is very much at the core of their practices and so it is important for you to understand how it is that you relate to your Gods and how you may wish to develop that relationship. Say to yourself "will joining this group benefit that relationship?"

Standing with the Clan

When you join a group such as a Coven, Grove or Hearth, you are not just taking a step in developing your beliefs, you are also taking a step into the lives of other people and they also move into your life. In many ways this can be like gaining an extended family. You will be sharing some very intimate moments with these people, allowing their ideas to help shape your own and teaching each other as you go. In a more mundane sense, you will most likely eat alongside them at times, drink together and maybe even go away to places with them. So obviously it is very important that you actually like these people! It doesn't really matter whether or not they share your beliefs and you like their practices, if you can't stand being around them. A religious or ritual group can be just like any other. It has good times and bad. The people are like a family that can support and guide each other, but they can also disagree and gossip amongst themselves as much as anyone else. Each group will be as different and unique as its members and the dynamic between them. You need to take into account how you would fit into that dynamic and indeed, they need to know that they will get along with you too.

Benefits of working in a group:
- Coming together for the sake of worshiping the Gods and performing magic is an ancient practice that has been performed across many cultures for thousands of years. By joining a group you are following in the footsteps this tradition.
- There is a common belief that working in a group, especially in rituals and magic, raises more energy to put into those rituals, making a group stronger than a solitary practitioner.
- Some paths emphasize the importance of honouring family and the community. Working in a group helps to keep one mindful to this ideal.
- Being part of a group often gives you access to personal teachers and guides to help you on your path.
- In religions such as Wicca, there are specific teachings that can only be obtained through initiating into a Coven.
- As you become more experienced in a group you will gain the opportunity to become a teacher in that group yourself.
- Working in a group provides close friends and family that you can share your beliefs with.

In the words of one Gardnerian Wiccan Priestess:

> *"I prefer to work as part of a group rather than alone because it gives me a sense of "family" and of a group mind and energy. We have shared experiences, which have occurred as a group, and also individual experiences that others within the group have also experienced at one time or other and we are able to discuss these things and explore them as a group. Above all, it is a connection to the wider Wiccan family and the support that this brings, which makes group work preferable to solitary work for me."*

Standing Alone

Unlike many religions in our culture which put an emphasis on coming together as a group, Pagan religions generally don't require this. In fact, due to the scattered spread of Pagans it is often just the easier option for an individual to practice alone and in many cases this is the preferred way for them to do things. Being solitary can make things difficult in a lot of ways, but it can also have its own unique benefits. You can do things exactly how you want and only need worry about yourself. On the downside, though, you don't have the benefit of learning from other people, other than what you may read in books or maybe on the internet. This in itself can be a problem, as you won't necessarily know which websites are on the level, which books are good and where their authors are coming from. But of course, being solitary doesn't mean that you suddenly can't talk to other Pagans at all. You're just as welcome to attend Pagan events and join certain organisations.

Ultimately the solitary path is about freedom! It leaves a person free to find their own way, find their own truths and make their own mistakes. To be solitary is to learn the hard way, but also to reap all the benefits of doing all the work yourself. As a solitaire, you may lack the support and guidance of other people, but you take the direct path to inner strength and individuality.

Benefits of working as a Solitaire:
- Following a solitary Pagan path gives you the freedom to find your own way without having to follow a structured method of progressing.
- A lot of solitaries are Eclectic, meaning that they take bits and pieces from a lot of different paths in order to build their own. This is a lot harder to do in a group.
- Some people choose the solitary path simply as a matter of privacy. To them, their spirituality is their business and they don't feel comfortable sharing it.
- When you work alone you don't need to worry about attending group functions, meaning that you can essentially set your own time-table and do things wherever you like.
- Rituals performed by the solitaire are like a reflection of that person. As there is no one else to influence their workings, they are free to give all their rituals a personal touch.
- Coming before the Gods alone, the solitaire is solely responsible for how they present themselves.
- Some people just don't work well with others.

In the words of a solitary witch:

> *"I've practiced alone for many years now and enjoy the freedom it gives me to explore my spirituality. I've enjoyed doing some rituals with close friends occasionally, but this also helps me realise that everyone is moving at their own rate and so practicing alone most of the time has allowed me to move at my own rate without worrying about those around me who may be either playing catch-up or perhaps just have interests that steer them away from the direction that I want to go in."*

Despite the differences between these two styles of spirituality, it is important to note that choosing one does not necessarily negate the use of the other. A member of a group can still practice things alone in their own time and in their own way, and a solitaire may choose to work with others from time to time, assuming she can find people interested in doing so.

Advice on working alone

The greatest problem faced by any solitary practitioner is the need for information. Ultimately how you experience magic and the Gods will be entirely unique to you, but there are methods and techniques already in place that most will want to use in order to follow their chosen path. After all, that is a lot easier than trying to invent your entire religious path from scratch (though there is nothing to stop you from doing so) and chances are that it is the already established ideas of your chosen path that attracted you to it in the first place. The problem after that point is in finding information that allows you to move beyond the basics and into a detailed, accurate practice. So the best thing to do is read as many books as you can get your hands on and talk to other practitioners to share information and ideas. Find out who the most reputable authors are in your area of interest and the ones to stay away from.

Sooner or later though, you may just have to realise that there is some information and experiences that you just can't get if you work alone. In fact, some paths (Wicca, for example) have oath-bound information which is held in secret and can only be released to people who are initiated into an official group. But that doesn't invalidate the solo path. Indeed, as a solitary practitioner you may also have experiences that are entirely unique to you and maybe even gain your own private practices and insights. Likewise, you are free to just disregard any traditional teachings and practices that don't agree with you. A group may insist on certain things in their rituals, but a solitaire can use whatever they like and just throw out the rest. In other words, your practices can be made entirely unique to you. The main guidance for a solitaire comes from two sources: Written material such as books and websites, and personal experience. Don't underestimate the value of either of these things, because you will have to use them to the fullest in order to progress.

Advice on Joining a Group

When joining a group there are generally four stages to building this relationship: Meeting, Learning, Initiation and Advancement.

Meeting
The first step to joining a group is the initial stage of seeking them out, getting in contact with them and communicating with them. The best way to find a group these days is probably online or by attending Pagan events. Good websites to use are:

Witchvox at http://www.witchvox.com
The Pagan Federation at http://www.paganfed.org

If you live in the UK then a good event to go to would be Witchfest or one of the many Pagan moots across the country, while international readers should check their online country listings for events in their areas. Both Witchvox and The Pagan Federation International will provide some event listings or ways to find groups in your area.

Initial communication may be through emails and phone calls, but eventually (assuming you are okay with the people so far) you will come to meet the group in person.

Always be careful when meeting people for the first time!!!

Meeting people is a big step and you must take care. Always meet in a public place, let people know where you will be and what you are doing, and if you are under eighteen get an adult to go with you, at least for the initial meeting.

At this stage you are getting to know the people in the group and they are getting to know you. This allows both you and them to find out whether or not you are right for each other. Keep it light, keep it social and you can move onto the heavier stuff later.

Learning
If you decide that you wish to go ahead with the group and they are happy to have you, then it is time to start discussing the deeper aspects of belief. This is when you will have to start learning in depth what they believe and how they practice.

At this stage you are still able to walk away if you find anything that you are unhappy with and indeed, you probably should. However, it is also important to remember that the group won't always cater to what you or any one member wants, which is why compromise is important at times. Be ready to compromise, but don't compromise over something you strongly disagree with. Many groups practice in certain ways that you may not be comfortable with. They may meet regularly every week, possibly perform rituals naked (skyclad), or maybe even use alcohol in rituals. If you don't agree with these or anything else, then don't join such a group.

However, the most important aspect of this stage is as preparation for Initiation. It is a time to learn all the basics of the group's beliefs so that you are ready to take the bigger step into official membership.

Initiation

Initiation can cover several different things in regards to our meaning here. There is literal Initiation into a group, involving a ritual, but for our purposes here "initiation" can also be something as simple as filling out an application or paying your membership dues. But for the sake of this article, we will look at the more literal kind of Initiation through the use of an official ritual. Initiation is the culmination of all your studies and the final result of your decision to commit to group practice. Depending on the religion or group you are joining, Initiation rituals can all be very different. In some paths it will be a process through which you declare yourself to your Gods, in others it will be process through which patron Gods actually choose you. More conventionally though, Initiation is primarily about being accepting into a group and declaring yourself as a follower of a certain path.

Perfect love and Perfect trust

This is a phrase that you may come across when dealing with groups and Initiations, especially in regards to witchcraft groups. It means a great deal of things and has many subtle levels, but it is a very good way of summing up what it means to be Initiated. When you are Initiated the Coven (or similar group) is making a declaration that they trust you with their secrets and that they are willing to accept you into their family. It is a sharing of things that are very intimate to them and it is also a great honour. By accepting Initiation you are proclaiming that you are indeed worthy of that trust and willing to trust them in the same way. For this reason it is very important that you are sure about taking this step. Initiation is a gift, a commitment and a responsibility. Thus, it is not to be taken lightly. For the same reason, you shouldn't rush into Initiation too soon. The kind of love and trust that is shared between

Initiates should be treated like any other important relationship. It takes time to build up that kind of connection to people and it is a bad idea to try to force it too soon. As an Initiate you are making a declaration to yourself, your Coven mates and to the Gods themselves. It is a declaration to not only enter the group in this spirit of perfect love and perfect trust, but also to strive to maintain that ideal throughout your life. So make sure that you are willing to accept everything that comes with such a commitment.

The Self-Initiation Fable

"Self-initiation" is technically an incorrect term, but it is one that you may run into from time to time. Initiation is a gift of acceptance. To be Initiated means that a group that you don't belong to is welcoming you into their fold. It is the opening of a door by another person and inviting you to step through. You couldn't declare yourself a Catholic Priest and you couldn't give yourself a Knighthood. Initiation is the same; it is something that other people give to you, not something that you can give to yourself. What people often refer to as "self-Initiation" is more correctly termed as a Dedication. This is when a person in a solitary capacity declares that they are going to follow a certain path or certain Gods, often by performing a personal ritual. Dedication Rituals are absolutely fine for the solitary practitioner and a very good way to give your path a sense of personal meaning and structure, as well as an outspoken declaration to the Gods.

See below for an example of how to construct your own Dedication Ritual.

Advancement

Things don't just stop after Initiation. Some groups have very defined stages of advancement that Initiates can follow, but even if they don't you still continue to advance, as the very nature of being in such a group means that you will continue to gain experiences and knowledge. Some groups are specifically geared towards teaching and even network with other groups in order to expand their field of knowledge. Indeed, many group members will even study in areas beyond the central teachings of the group they belong to, working with the practices of other Pagan religions and spiritualities.

So even if you join a group, it isn't a closed door that restricts you to the ideas and beliefs of that group. Chances are that the group itself will encourage further study from its members in the hope that the entire group will reap the benefits. In this way we begin to see how group practice can provide a person with access to a larger and more varied assortment of information, while also giving them a focused insight to their central beliefs.

Merry Meet and Merry Part

If you are lucky you may find a group that helps keep you happy and spiritually fulfilled for the rest of your life. But chances are that eventually you and your fellow Initiates will part company.

The reasons for this can be many. People move house, decide to start their own groups, seek independence or perhaps change beliefs altogether and feel that they need to walk a new path. Most of the time any group will wish their friends luck if they have to leave, though they will obviously be missed. But we can't overlook the fact that sometimes people do also part on bad terms. Obviously, nobody wants to find themselves in this situation, so the best way to avoid it is to be as sure as you can about a group before you join. Make sure their goals are compatible with yours and perhaps more importantly, that you and your perspective coven-mates will get along as friends. Remember, you are likely to be spending a lot of time with these people, so make sure that you enjoy their company.

If and when it does come time to leave the group yourself, leave with the same spirit of perfect love and perfect trust that you came into the group with. When you leave you take with you the trust and secrets of those you leave behind and they hold the same of you. So be sure to keep the promises you made and in so doing keep the friends and family that you made also. As the saying goes: Merry meet, merry part and merry meet again.

Example of a Dedication Ritual

A Dedication Ritual can be performed by the solitary practitioner to mark the beginning of their newly chosen path. Usually this is declaration to your chosen Gods, but can also be used in a general sense to give yourself a personal milestone that represents some kind of new spiritual beginning in your life. The following is a guideline for how you can create your own Dedication Ritual and shape it to fit your own spiritual path.

Create Sacred Space
Before you begin your ritual, you will need to decide where you will perform it. This space should be clean, quiet and away from disturbances. This is also the place where you will set up any kind of altar that you wish to use in your ritual. Your altar will be a place where you can keep your tools and any other items that you feel are relevant. Some people may choose to place candles upon their altar to represent their deities. This ritual example will assume the use of such candles. Other common items are incense, food, magical tools, symbols, statues and pictures.

When your ritual area is prepared, it is customary to open your ritual by marking this area as Sacred Space. This is very often done by Casting a Circle, but it can also be done through the beating of a drum, singing, through meditation or by filling the space with cleansing incense or sprinkled water.

Call to the Gods
With your ritual space consecrated, it is time to call to your chosen Gods. This is not a summoning; it is an invitation in which you are respectfully requesting that your Gods honour you with their presence so that they can observe your Dedication. Invite each God/Goddess separately and do so in order of importance. If your path focuses on balance between the Gods, then call the feminine deities first, simply as a matter of common politeness. As you invite each deity to attend, light the candle set on your alter to represent them.

Call to others
Once all your Gods are called to attendance, you may now call to any other beings that you may wish to observe your ritual and bless you with their presence. This can include ancestor spirits, nature spirits, fae and angels.In some cases other being may already be in attendance as a result of Casting a Circle when creating your sacred space. For example, some traditions call upon Elementals and angels when they call the different quarters of a magic circle. If

this is the case then that is fine, this stage may still be used to call to any other beings that you would like to invite into your sacred space.

State your intention

When all attendees are called, it is time to declare you intention. The wording here should be a heartfelt announcement of why you are performing the ritual and what it is you hope to achieve on your path. This step is about possibilities. It is here that you explain why you want to follow this path and your acknowledgement that this is your first step on a new and unpredictable journey.

Symbolic Death

With your intentions announced, now you is the time to call an end to your old life so that you might start your journey. This is a symbolic representation of how you are about to change, like the caterpillar that becomes a butterfly, first you must put an end to who you have been in order to become who you wish to be. This "death" shows the ending of one stage of your existence.

Do not actually harm yourself! This is a symbolic death. Feel free to act this out or to just announce it, but whatever you do, don't put yourself in a position where you could actually damage yourself. This should be a beautiful and meaningful demonstration of how you are changing, not an opportunity to scar yourself or worse. Be sensible.

Swear your Oath

At this point you are in a state between the person you were and the person you are yet to become. You are a traveller ready for his journey, waiting to take his first step. You exist between two stages, the life that you have already symbolically ended and the new life that you have yet to begin. While in this death state this is the time to stand before your Gods and state your intentions, swearing your allegiance to a path that honours them. You are like a human soul undergoing judgement, your heart being weighed against the feather of truth. Show the Gods why you are worthy of their guidance and make a vow to honour your alignment to them.

Symbolic Rebirth

Now begins your new life. You are reborn under the guidance of the Gods and your journey starts anew. At this point in time some Traditions would have you given a magical name to mark your entrance into your new life. As such you can feel free to choose a magical name that is only used between you and your Gods. If you do choose to do this, then be sure to make your new name something truly meaningful. Don't just pick something because it sounds cool; instead take the time long before you begin the ritual so that you can put some serious spiritual thought into what you want this special name to be. Meditate on this point if you feel you are able. Magical names aren't for everyone though. Whether you choose to take one or not, use this part of the ritual to show you understand that your journey has begun and that you will honour the commitments you have already made. You are a new person now, reborn.

Give an offering

Show your appreciation to the Gods by making an offering. Obviously you would have this offering already prepared before the ritual. It can an offering of food, incense, flowers, music, or anything else that you feel would be pleasing to your new Gods. Do some research on your deities so that you can get an idea of the kind of things that best apply to them. Remember, this stage of the ritual is a gift from you to the divine. You have invited them in; they have honoured you with their presence and accepted you as a Dedicant. This is the point where you thank them for these things, so please take the time to make it meaningful. In this ritual you are forging a new relationship with your Gods, taking them on as guides, parents, friends and confidants. Use this part of the ritual to show gratitude for all these things.

Toast

Okay, so you have just started the great adventure of your spiritual journey, it's time to celebrate! Make a toast to your new beginning and celebrate your relationship with your deities. Take a drink* and if you really feel like it you can even dance around a little.

*Keep in mind the legal age of alcohol consumption. If you are underage, don't worry, you can toast just as well with fruit juice. Grape juice can make a good substitute for wine.

Thank and dismiss attendees

With the festivities over, it's time to thank your guests and bid them farewell. It's customary to dismiss attendees in order of importance. Thank the Gods for coming to preside over your ritual and bid them goodbye. As you allow each God/Goddess to depart extinguish their corresponding candle as well. Next dismiss everyone else you invited, working in the same order as when you called them.

Clear the Sacred Space.

You are the only person present once more. The ritual has come to an end and now it is time to draw it to a close. If you cast a Circle, now is the time to close it. If you did anything else to create sacred space for your ritual, then use an appropriate way to settle it back to normal. This could be something as simple as ringing a bell, letting the smell of incense clear the air or possibly singing a new song or chant to mark the closing of the ritual. Some people will choose to leave their altar set up permanently from now on as a marker of their new path. This is fine, but keep in mind that unattended candles and incense are a fire risk, so don't leave them burning when you aren't there.

The Truth of the Matter

A lot of people talk about being solitary or being in a group, as if it is an either/or situation, but the reality of the matter is that the majority of Pagans seem to do both. Pagans who only practice alone or only practice in their group appear to be in the minority. In actuality, most Pagans, whether they belong to a group or not, still practice alone and the majority of those that mainly practice alone still join other people at open rituals, conferences, moots and so on. For a great many Pagans, their time between group and solo practice, tends to fall about even.

So what's better?

Is it better to work alone or to work in a group? Quite honestly, there is no "better," there is only what is better for you. Some people naturally gravitate towards one or the other, some try both before deciding and some don't get much choice in the matter because of where they live or the people around them. The important thing is to do what you feel comfortable with. Paganism isn't about indoctrination. Nobody is going to force you to join a group, but people will most likely help you if you try to find one for yourself. Just keep close to what feels right and practice in the way that you find is best. Your spirituality is your own, so walk the path that feels right for you.

Pagan Generation

Building a Pagan Practice

Depending on the Pagan Path you feel drawn to, you will find different things of importance to you in constructing your style of practice. There are already many great books out there that will be able to fill you with inspiration and advice on your path, so I'll not try and cram every detail of each path into this single chapter. Instead, we'll now take a look at many of the common elements, items and practices that unite many Pagans, regardless of path, and which you may find useful in building your pagan practice.

Altar

For many modern Pagans, their altar is the heart of their Paganism. It stands not only as somewhere that they can practice their faith, but also as a point of sacred space within their home. Those who are lucky enough to have the extra space, may even allocate a significant area or room to house their altar and to act as a kind of spiritual sanctuary or temple, where they can step away from the mundane world and let all their worldly troubles melt away. The idea of "sacred space" is very important to many Pagans and construction of an altar is one of the most fundamental uses of sacred space that is common to many Pagans, both modern and ancient. The ancient Greeks and Romans would have sacred altars or shrines where they would honour certain Gods and the spirits of their homes. Likewise, the ancient Germanic peoples would very often have special spaces or buildings for housing shrines to their Gods. As modern Pagans we can take up these kinds of traditions.

But what is an altar used for?

A shrine or altar serves many purposes. Fundamentally, it is perhaps best seen as a meeting place where worlds can ceremonially come together. A place we can go to in order to feel closer to our Gods, our ancestors and the spiritual world around us. Of course, we don't necessarily need an altar or shrine in order to connect with the spiritual world, but it does play an important role in a functional and ceremonial sense. Our homes are extensions of ourselves. They are the manifestation of our individuality, our families and the lives we live. Having that altar space in our homes can help us to create a constant physical presence for our spirituality, in a similar way to how the other objects in our homes are a physical extension of those other things that are important to us. But more than this, an altar also serves a functional purpose, as a place where we can make offerings, conduct rituals and for some Pagans, perform magic.

Having an altar helps us manifest our spirituality in the physical world. It is a meeting place between the physical and spiritual, and quickly because the spiritual heart of the home.

Statues

Statuary and images of the Gods can play a very important part in the practices of many Pagans. Such things can make prominent features upon an altar, or in themselves serve as shrines throughout the home and even in your garden. A witch may, for example, have a statue of their Goddess and/or God upon their altar, which then become a part of their practices and an additional focus for their workings. A Hellenist, on the other hand, may have statues of the Greek Gods throughout their home, serving various functions. For example, a statue of the Goddess Hecate may be placed at the doorway of the house to guard it, in accordance with ancient custom.

Statues, reliefs and images of the Gods can be quite easily found these days, either from Pagan or New Age shops, or online. Today's Pagan has many advantages when it comes to gathering items like these for their faith, as Paganism has a greater commercial presence now than it did in the first decades of the modern Pagan revival. With such availability, there comes a great deal of choice. If you're going to buy statues for your practice, shop around and see what's out there. The best advice that can be given here, is probably to couple your purchases with some research. If you are going to buy a statue of a God or Goddess, then find out about that Goddess. Learn who they are, what they stand for, where they come from. You'll likely find that knowing these kinds of things will add a new dimension to practices and make your statue much more meaningful.

Of course, when it comes to adding meaning to your statue or image, you may want to consider making it yourself. While there are many wonderful statues and images out there to buy, taking the time to carve, paint or sculpt your own can be all the more wonderful. Doing this, you not only end up with something that is entirely unique to you and your practices, but you also have devoted time, effort towards an act of faith, which means that your artwork is as much a gift to the Gods as it is to yourself. You may even be surprised at the money you can save by taking this approach. Canvasses and paints can be bought very cheaply at discount shops, while air-dry clay can be bought at most hobby shops. Another form of art that you could consider is pyrography, which involves burning designs into wood or leather. Pyrography pens can be bought cheaply either online or from a hobby shop, while decent wood is always available in the form of bread boards, which can be easily bought for next to nothing. You'll then also have a tool that you can reuse.

If you choose to use statues or images in your practices, then there is a wide array of options open to you. Explore what's available and go with whatever speaks to you.

Jewellery

Jewellery, as a personal expression of faith, is common to a great many world religions and Paganism is no different. While it is unlikely that jewellery will play a very central part in your actual practices, it nonetheless can be very significant. Wearing a pentacle, Mjolnir (Thor's Hammer), or triquetra (a three-fold European design), for example, is a way of showing your faith and keeping a symbol of it with you. There is, of course, no need for anyone to declare their religion to the world or dangle it in people's faces, in fact you're quite likely to annoy people if you do, but jewellery, like a ring or necklace, can have great personal meaning. What we wear is an expression of who we are and our faith is part of that, so it is understandable that many religious people (including Pagans) feel moved to express their faith in what they wear.

Candles

Candles are in no way a necessity, but let's face it, they are very useful! I think that a lot of Pagans would agree that there is almost something magical in the lighting of a candle. The act somehow embodies a feeling of tradition and "otherness", whether it's lighting a candle upon your altar or lighting candles on a birthday cake. As the latter example may call to mind, the extinguishing of a candle can also have that sense of magic and tradition.

Candles are often used in ritual, regardless of how essential they may or may not be to a particular Pagan path. In some instances, candles can be the centre of entire rituals or magical systems, such as Candle Burning Magic.
If nothing else, candles create a unique ambiance, which helps us to enter into the mentality of the sacred. Lighting a candle is not a everyday act in the modern world, so it is immediately something out of the norm, that allows us to begin the process of separation from the mundane.
Plus, being practical, candle also provide light in a way that feels more appropriate than electric lighting and if you are working outdoors, candles may be the only viable form of light that you can use.

Safety First: Please remember to take care when using a naked flame, both indoors and outdoors. They are fire hazards and we wouldn't want to be responsible for starting a fire in our homes, a woodland or anywhere else. So never leave candles burning unattended and always make sure that they are extinguished when you are finished.

Incense

Like candles, incense may not be essential to your path, though again, it is useful. Some paths will place a higher importance on the use of incense than others will. Traditionally, in many forms of Paganism (and world religions in general), incense is used as a form of offering, made to the Gods or certain spirits. Frankincense is a common incense used in this way, but if you are seeking to make an offering of incense to a certain deity, you may want to do a little research, as many deities were/are traditionally considered to be associated with different incenses, which are perhaps more appropriate as offerings for them.

Additionally, incenses can be blended together for certain tasks. Incense is usually derived from various plants, oils and resins. In certain systems of Paganism and magic, these plants, oils and resins are seen to be associated with certain concepts. Some may be seen as connected to certain Gods, others may be seen as good for particular health issues, some may have astrological connections, while others may be identified as connected with concepts like money, law and love. So it is common for practitioners using incense to create their own unique incense recipes geared towards a certain purpose, by combining different incenses based on their associations. For example, a combination of rose, clove and allspice could be used as an incense for being lucky in love.

In the early days of your practice, you may find it easier to buy pre-made incense combinations or "joss sticks" for a certain purpose. Once you feel comfortable in your practice, you might like to move on to incense oils and begin to mix different ones for your own purposes. Then, when you feel secure in your knowledge of different plants, herbs and resins, and what they are associated with, you may wish to begin buying raw resin and dried plants, so that you can mix up your own recipes for burning on charcoal blocks (which can be bought in shops or online). Perhaps if your knowledge of nature is sufficient, you may begin to go out and collect your own plant extracts to be dried and added to your various recipes.

Mixing up recipes of incense like this is yet another way to individualise your practice. However, to get you started, there are a fair few books on the market that contain incense recipes and explanations of the qualities associated with different incenses.

Safety First: Just like with candles, incense involves the use of flame. Never leave burning incense unattended and make sure that it is fully extinguished before discarding. It is easy enough to see when a joss stick is finished and safe, but when using other forms of incense, you must take extra care. If you are using oil and there is some left, the oil could still be hot! This is doubly important with charcoal blocks, as they will remain incredibly hot long after your incense has finished burning and even if they look burnt out. A charcoal block that has finished burning, will crumble to dust easily, but a charcoal block that merely looks like it's finished could still have a red-hot core. If you are working with charcoal blocks, give them a couple of hours before discarding, just to make sure that they are no longer hot. If you are in a rush and outdoors, you may want to pour some water on them, just to make sure.

Books

There's really no escaping that sooner or later you'll find it useful to pick up a book or two about the kind of Paganism you're interested in. Of course, there are other useful tools out there that can help you find your way, such as websites and e-groups, but these really can't take the place of a good book. The advantage of a book is that while it may, in many cases, express the views of the author, you can look around and find out how well a particular book is regarded by those that follow the same path as you. One easy way of doing this is by looking at the customer reviews on websites that sell the book, such as Amazon.com, or by asking your fellow Pagans on an internet forum. Many Pagan magazines will also do book reviews. But of course, all opinions should be taken with a pinch of salt. Ultimately, it is for you to determine what you think of a book and how much it can aid you in your path.

Work Books

One of the most useful things that you can have, is a blank work book. This can be used for many things. Wiccans may use it as a Book of Shadows, or it could be used to record your various incense recipes, record your rituals, take notes on divinations, perhaps even a dream diary. While certainly not essential, a blank work book can have a hundred different uses.

Offering Bowl

You might find it useful to have a special offering bowl or plate, for making sacrifices to your Gods and/or spirits. This needn't be anything fancy, but it should be something special. That is to say that it should really be something dedicated to that purpose and that purpose alone, where possible. This is simply an act of reverence and adds to the meaning of the offering. Keeping it at your altar or shrine also helps add to the meaning and feel of that sacred space.

The use of an offering bowl or plate is simple. It is essentially a vessel for receiving offerings to your deities, ancestors, spirits, etc. You could pour into it libations (liquid offerings), such as wine or oil, or it could hold offerings of food. Ordinarily, such offerings would be returned to nature or in the case of libations, they would be poured directly onto the earth. But when practising indoors, an offering bowl becomes a good way of performing these tasks until you are able to place them outside. In some cases, offerings are supposed to be made in the home anyway, such as when making a sacrifice to household spirits. These offerings can be transferred outside later.

Ritual Dress

Wearing robes or other ritual garments is very popular among modern Pagans and there are an increasing number of suppliers that cater to this need. You may feel that a particular style of dress, such as ritual robes, may or may not be necessary. But either way, making the change into some form of special clothing can be a good way to further separate yourself from the mundane and feel closer to your spirituality. Quite a lot of people actually make their own ritual clothing, which again, is a great way to cut down costs while simultaneously adding that personal, unique touch to your spiritual path.

Tools of the Craft

Witchcraft has become very popular these days and many young people moving into Paganism are seeking to reclaim the power of this ancient art. The most common form of modern witchcraft has been inspired by Wicca and as such, a lot of this guide will explore this side of witchcraft, but we will also look into some of the ways these tools may be used outside of Wicca.

There are many different tools that are used in modern witchcraft, all with many layers of subtle meaning behind them. Understanding these tools, how they are used and the meaning behind them is the key to being a witch. Here we will explore these tools and how you can utilise them to your needs.

The Altar
Of all the ritual tools belonging to a witch, perhaps none is as important as the altar. The altar serves as the centre of ritual and acts as an area of sacred space for a witches workings. Sacred Space means many different things to many people and can also take on new meaning at different times. In regards to an altar, Sacred Space is a place that you have set aside for the placement of all other tools. If the witch were an office worker, then the altar would be her desk. It is the objects upon the altar that are used in ritual, but the altar forms the base that makes them special. When we make an altar it is a conscious act in which we declare that we are witches and that the items upon our altar are precious to us. If we were to just leave our magical tools scattered about the house or kept under our bed in a show-box, then they lose some of their reverence. But by placing them upon an altar, we give to them a position of status, declaring that they mean something to us and that any magical work we do with these tools has just as much meaning.

There are many different kinds of altar. Some are used to make offerings to the Gods, some are used as meditation centres, some as workplaces for communing with the other worlds. Our altar is for magic.

Altars can be permanent or temporary, but either way it is important to maintain their meaning. Just as rituals tools are shown to be meaningful by having a place on our altar, so too do we show the altar to be meaningful by placing it somewhere special. Some people like to have an entire room for rituals, in which they build a permanent altar. But for those among us who don't have that kind of space, we may simply place our altar in an area that already has some special, personal meaning to us, like the privacy of our bedrooms. While a lot of people choose their altar placement based on their personal beliefs, such as feng shui, cardinal directions or astrology.

The Athamé (Pronounced: A-the-may)

The Athamé is a dagger-like knife (traditionally with a black handle) used to represent and focus the personal power of the witch. As a projection of power it is commonly used to draw the Circle that surrounds ritual space. The Athamé itself is a symbol of power, used to direct the will of the wielder. It is associated with the element of Fire and is also a symbol of the universal masculine.

The Wand

The witch's wand is used in a similar way to the Athamé, for the purposes of directing the will of the witch. However, the wand is associated with the element of Air, and so is more effective for the focus of higher thoughts. But the main difference between the Athamé and the wand is that the Athamé is a weapon, thusly a symbol of protection and force. However, the wand is a symbol of the witch's status and shows that she has the power to direct her will and commune with the higher planes.

The Chalice

The element of Water is represented through the use of the Chalice, which is a ceremonial drinking vessel. The Chalice is used to take drinks during rituals and at the culmination of ritual work. In some paths it is also used to toast the Gods. This tool also represents the universal feminine or the womb, especially when combined with the Athamé during the symbolic Great Rite.

The Pentacle

Completing the main tools associated with the Elements is the Pentacle, which is the tool aligned with Earth. The Pentacle is a flat board or circle that is usually inscribed with a pentagram (a five-pointed star), though they may also have many other symbols upon them. This tool acts like a platform upon which many other acts are often performed – especially consecrations. It is symbolic of the Element of Earth, not only as the general Element, but also as the planet Earth itself and on a larger scale it can even be used as a symbol of the universe.

These items make up the core tools of the witch, each representing one of the mystical elements. All of these are commonly found upon a witches alter during rituals, if not all the time. However, there are also other tools that serve specific uses, as opposed to the broader tools already mentioned. Some of these are common to Wicca, but can also be found in the rituals of non-Wiccan witches, too.

The Bailine

This tool is sometimes referred to as the white handled knife, as that is the form it traditionally takes. The Bailine is a blade, but unlike the Athamé it serves a more practical purpose to the witch. As a part of rituals it is often used for cutting food either during or after magical workings. In addition, the Bailine is used by the witch to carve sigils, Runes, and other symbols into her other tools and similar relevant items. Sometimes it is also used to carve the tools themselves, by shaping the wood used for a wand or staff (such as the specific ceremonial staff, known as the Stang).

The Cauldron

Cauldrons and similar vessels have been prominent in several European mythologies, where they are often seen as magical items. To the witch, her Cauldron represents the divine feminine and the womb of creation. Some witches may use their Cauldron for scrying, while others will find a more mundane use for it by using it to mix consecrated water which is used to bless the Circle and those in attendance. If you are lucky enough to have a full sized Cauldron, then you can even feel free to cook a nice broth that can be shared and eaten to regain your strength after more exuberant rituals. For more Heathen orientated witches (those following a Germanic path), the Cauldron can be used as an excellent Glódhker, which is a type of fire-pot. In this use it represents Muspellsheimr, the first place to exist and the realm of cosmic fire.

The Bell

A small bell is common among some traditions. The bell is often used to signify the completing of a ritual or spell and some witches also use it to mark the casting of their Circle and the opening of their Circle afterwards. You don't necessarily need a real bell; there are witches who create their bell by lightly tapping their Athamé against the side of a metal chalice, thus creating the pleasant ring of a bell. Victorian spiritualist would sometimes use the tinkling of a small bell to call spirits near to them and some witches still use this method when attempting to work with spirits, especially on Samhain. Some say that the fae are also attracted to the pleasant sound of a bell.

The Besom

Also known as a broomstick, the Besom is the ultimate in stereotypical witchery!Traditionally, the Besom has two main uses to the witch. Firstly it is a tool for cleaning, used in the preparation of ritual space, simultaneously sweeping away dust and unwanted energies from where you intend to work. This practice goes back at least as far as ancient Egypt where priests would sweep clean their ritual space in much the same way as modern witches do. Secondly it is used in some rituals to represent a doorway, either between two worlds or between one stage of life and another. In this way it can be laid upon the border of the Circle, temporarily making a space where outsiders may come into the Circle, symbolically moving from one world into another.

The Sword

This particular tool is *generally* only used in groups and not by solitary witches. Like the Athamé it can be used to direct power and cast the Circle, but it is important that one doesn't come to think of it as a kind of scaled up Athamé. No, the Sword possesses its own meaning that places it as a unique tool in its own right. Swords have long been items that denote status, being as they were generally only carried by nobility. As such, the only person who wields a ritual Sword will usually be a High Priest or High Priestess, depending on the ritual and who is running it. Whereas all the other tools are items used to focus the personal power of the individual, the sword is a focal point for the entire Coven, representing the task being undertaken and the collective will of those trying to achieve it, and held by the person who is overseeing the endeavour.

The things that haven't been mentioned

The magical tools already mentioned are among those that you are most likely to encounter in witchcraft, however, this is not a list of all the tools a witch may need. Some Traditions may have certain tools that are more relevant to their practices, such as Magic Cords, Robes, a Scourge, perhaps even instruments like drums. But unless you join such a Tradition, there probably won't be much need for you to use these things, unless you personally wish to. Feel free to research them yourself and see how they make you feel.

Things we cant afford not to mention

Despite all these fancy names and special items, there are some tools that are so mundane that they may almost be forgotten in a list such as this. However, they are by no means any less important and in some cases they may even be more important. A witch must always be prepared, which is why it is a good idea to make sure that you always have a healthy stock of the following things:

Candles

Candles serve so many functions in witchcraft that they may actually be one of the most significant tools we have. They are used to represent the Gods, mark the corners of the Circle, work magic directly or even just to provide ambient lighting for a ritual. Indeed, if you have no candles then you are missing one of the most versatile tools in witchcraft.

Incense

Like candles, incense can also serve many purposes. Some people find it helps them meditate, some offer it up to the Gods, it can also be used in cleansing rituals and Banishings, plus some believe that certain aromas have mystical or medicinal properties. Don't forget an incense burner or censer, too.

Candlesticks

I'm not sure this needs too much explanation. If you have candles then you will need somewhere to put them. Many people buy or make special candlesticks for the purposes of holding God and Goddess candles during rituals.

A Bowl

Strange as it may sound, a good bowl can work wonders. It has obvious functional properties, such as holding the food for after workings, but a bowl can also be filled with many other useful things. When filled with water the bowl becomes a magic mirror. When filled with offerings it becomes a dedication to the Gods. When filled with salt water it can be used in consecration, preparation and dedication rituals. Oh, and while we are on the subject, keeping some water and salt handy is also a good idea.

A place to practice

It's not a lot of good getting together all your tools and preparing a ritual or spell if you don't have anywhere to perform it. A lot of witches like to practice outdoors in natural environments, but it is just as acceptable to practice in your own house. Some people even prefer it.

A torch

Not really a ritual tool, but if you are planning on practising outdoors in the dark, having a torch with you will help ensure that you make it to the ritual. Although, if this is how you choose to practice, please be careful. Its great to get close to nature, but it might not be a good idea to be walking around the woods on your own in the middle of the night. At the very least, let people know where you are and where possible never go alone.

A warm coat

Seriously, it can get freezing outdoors.

Your concentration

You are always the most important part of any ritual or magical working. Without you there is no magic, so make sure that you keep your mind in your workings. The witch must be focused, disciplined and aware.

A Word on Witchcraft

All of the tools written about above are generally focused towards a style of Witchcraft that is inspired by Wicca. This is because it is the most common style of Witchcraft in modern Paganism. However, there are many other kinds of Witchcraft, including Hedgewitchery, Traditional Folk Witchcraft, and others. If you think that these may interest you, then feel free to look them up. You may even find that you mix and match elements of many different styles of Witchcraft.

Make magic!

Okay, so now you have the information you need to get under way as a witch. All you need to do now is gather your tools and learn to use them. Just try to keep in mind that the tool itself holds no power. They are just things. The power comes from within you and the tools allow you to direct that power. They are a way to channel your energies and focus your mind towards making the connection between your will and the universe.

Learn what your tools represent, establish a personal connection to them and they will become an extension of yourself. With this, they will allow you to reach out into the unseen worlds and explore the mysteries of reality.

Pagan Generation

A Theory of Magic

When I began thinking about what it would entail to try and write this chapter, I really didn't envy myself of the task ahead of me. Magic is such a varied and dynamic medium that views and practices of it differ greatly among magic users. I decided the best and fairest way to go about this was to go back to basics, so I dug through my books, searching for the common threads of magic and the most popular views of it. Between the classic occultists, modern witchcraft and traditional magical lore, I found certain common threads that I hope to convey through the medium of my own perspective and the perspective of the greater magical community. Some beliefs and ideas may get lost in the shuffle and for that, I apologise. But the attempt here is not to produce an all-inclusive guide to magic around the world. No, that would require a book in its own right. Instead, what is presented here is a fundamental view of the central ideas that persist most commonly among the different schools of magical thought. Hopefully, from there, these basic ideas can be easily integrated into your own magical practices and grant you a better understanding of how they work and why you do them.

What is Magic?

When depicted in movies and TV shows, magic often appears as some kind of incredible power, force or energy that is utterly unique to anything that exists. That is not the case. Magic isn't about summoning some kind of alien power into existence; it is instead about influencing those energies which already exist, both known and unknown. The famed occultist Aleister Crowley described his brand of magic as:

"...the science and art of causing Change in conformity with Will."

Indeed, even today this remains one of the most popular and accurate descriptions of magic (or Magick, as Aleister put it) that is used. But this in itself does not necessarily help the novice to determine what magic actually *is*. For Crowley every intentional act was a magical act, but here in this chapter we will focus on magic as defined beyond the realms of the mundane and ordinary. However, we have our launching point into magic: "Causing Change in conformity with Will".

When asking many magical practitioners what magic is and how it works, the most common answer that I have encountered is that it is the manipulation of the Energies around us in order to affect the Universe as we desire. This too, is a good definition. But without a little context, it is utterly meaningless. Turning on your television affects the flow of electrical energy and results in you watching the show you want. But we would hardly consider this an act of magic. That is just technology at work. But magicians and witches have ways and means for accessing and manipulating energies in ways that require more than technology, as the energies at play are often beyond the current scope of technology. But in order to place some meaning to these words we must first understand what these "Energies" are and in order to do that we must dip into the general worldview of a typical magic user.

The attitude towards the workings of magic more often reflects the spiritual perceptions of the user. That is to say, the magic works because they first have an understanding of the Universe on a magical level. This in no way implies some kind of in-born insight into the cosmos. Religions around the world, for the most part, have the same view of reality – that it is composed of different aspects, levels or dimensions. As a sweeping statement that appears to be fundamentally wrong and I will be the first to admit that there are definitely exceptions to the rule, but in the broad spectrum of world belief it is certainly true to say. Whether you follow a Celtic tradition, Wicca, Christianity or an indigenous tribal religion, the idea that there are aspects of reality that exist beyond the immediate physical one are more or less universal. All accept the existence (or in some cases the illusion) of the physical universe. But beyond that is the idea that there are also various Etheric levels of reality, such as the spiritual, mental, astral, etc. These aspects of our reality exist alongside the physical and in some instances can and do interact with our physical reality. The common belief also persists that human beings (and perhaps other living things) have as part of us, the ability or a natural connection, that allows us access to these realms in a limited way.

When we speak of "Energies" we are speaking of the Etheric forces that comprise reality on all levels. So now when we regard the idea of manipulating Energies and causing change in conformity to will, we are talking about the ability to access and exert our will upon the Universe at different levels.

That is magic.

But this is not a simple act of saying "I want to summon a spirit" by means of affecting the spiritual plain of reality. No, Magic goes beyond desire and into action. So in order to bring about what we desire, we must use the right tool for the job.

Think of it this way: If we wish to achieve something in the physical world, as physical beings it is often simpler to just do it ourselves and in a physical way. Toasters are good for making toast, shovels are good for digging holes and pens are good for writing. But we wouldn't use a pen to make toast or a toaster to dig a hole. In the same way, our technology and science which operates so well for the physical world isn't a very good tool for accessing and controlling the spiritual and astral levels of reality. The right tool for the right job. So, we use magic as our science and magical tools used in the right way to bring out our results.

Thinking of magic as a science sets us on the right track to performing it and like all sciences, we must understand it in order to use it properly. After all, nobody splits the atom by accident; you need to know what you are doing first. Magic requires understanding in order to reap the best results. The better you understand what you are doing, the more likely you are to achieve your aims. This is why just picking up a spell book in a shop and reading out the words is just folly. I'm not going to saying anything against the fine authors who have gone to the trouble provide spells, formulas and rituals for us in their books, but I will note that unless you understand the theory behind these things, it isn't likely to do anything particularly great for you.

Magic, as an art and science, reaches through several different mediums simultaneously. It is spiritual, psychological, sometimes religious, physical, etc. and it is through understanding the interplay of these things that we get our best results. When using a ritual knife in magic, we are performing a physical act, a religious act and a psychological act, all with the intention of a spiritual benefit. But although we can read in a book what to physically do with the knife, unless you recognise the psychological and religious implications of what you are doing, along with the spiritual nature of the intent, you are still only using a small part what is needed to work its magic.

Magic works on many different levels, passing through the spectrum of the different planes of our universe. So when we perform magic, it is proper to understand how what we do, think, feel and believe touches the different levels of reality and directs our magical workings towards what we desire to achieve.

Interconnection

For many ages now, one of the primary concepts across Mysticism has been that of the interconnectivity of all things. This is one of many mystic truths that modern science is now beginning to understand on a theoretical level and show through experimentation. However, Mystics and magic users have long been aware of the interconnectivity of our reality. Interconnection is the idea that all things are in some way connected on some fundamental level and that by affecting one thing in the right way, we can affect other things that may seem unrelated. This idea tends to manifest in one of two ways, either in the idea that all things are connected like links in a chain, or that what we perceive as separation is really an illusion and that in reality all things are essentially the same thing.

These concepts can be difficult for us to wrap our minds around, but across the globe they remain prevalent in many magical traditions. Through actions and events that appear irrelevant to the casual observer, we can focus our minds to direct the energies across the chain of our interconnected reality in order to bring about the effects we desire.

Using both the idea of an interconnected reality and that a universe which exists on many levels, we have produced the foundation for how magic works within our universe. Everything in our universe is all at once connected to everything else and exists on many levels. Through ritual and spell-work we may access the different levels of our universe, direct the energies that we have accessed and then send them out to affect the universe in another way, like ripples in a pond.

By manipulating the energies on one level of reality and setting them to a purpose, we start a pattern of change into motion through which we have made a fundamental impact on the universe itself. Each level touches upon all others and the energies flow naturally between all of them. By dipping your will into that flow we work in accordance with nature, setting the energies towards a pattern that conforms with our desires, flowing across the many planes of our universe to achieve our goal.

Indeed, it is important to note that among modern magicians the view of magic is that of something natural. Magic does not defy the fundamental laws of nature; it merely manipulates them to a degree. Magic users work in accordance with the natural flow of the universe, like the difference between redirecting the path of a river in comparison to making it flow up hill. The prior works *with* nature, while the latter would defy it.

Magical Tools

In the working of magic, magicians and witches use a wide variety of tools to help them work with the energies about them. These tools can be anything from blades, wands and spoken words, to music, dance and even martial arts. But why use tools at all?

As we speak of the different levels of reality, we use magical tools as a way to form a bridge between these different planes of existence. However, the tools themselves have no innate magical powers or abilities and even during magic, it is not the tools that are the bridges. No, the tools of magic are the means by which we ourselves become the bridge that opens up the flow of energies between the different levels of reality. Whether the tool is an athame or a wand, the item serves to open us up to the other aspects of ourselves. Human beings are connected to the many levels of reality that we have been discussing, as we are all at once physical, mental and spiritual beings. We have bodies, minds and souls. Most of the time we exist in a state where we live in the physical world and understand ourselves through our higher mental functions. But when we delve below this, slipping into our subconscious mind, we reach a point where we can access the deeper parts of ourselves and allow them to become expressed as readily as our physical selves. We can connect to the spiritual part of ourselves, the astral part of ourselves, the unconscious part of ourselves, etc. This is what the tools enable us to do.

Magical tools are chosen for their symbolism, which appeals to us on a subconscious level and equally on a religious/spiritual level. By understanding the hidden symbolism behind these things we are able to form a connection within ourselves by using those tools and in turn, the combination of many tools in a specific way creates a complex and purposeful connection within the user who understands them. In this way we achieve a unity of self in which all aspects of our being become represented simultaneously and so we as beings exist consciously through all levels of our reality. In short, we attain a total awareness of what we are and how we relate to the universe. With this conscious connection to the greater all, we can then gather and manipulate those energies that exist on these planes that are in and around us.

So we see, the tools of a witch/magician are not seen as some kind special item with in-built power, but instead they are a psychological aid that allows us to delve into the depths of our psyches and access the potential that truly exists within us.

Varieties of magic

When discussing the varieties of magic it is far too broad a subject to adequately sum up in this article. Even the magical practices of very close communities can vary greatly, even if they share many other traits either culturally or religiously. So instead we will look at varieties of magic in terms of magical goals and how they are achieved.

Evocation

Evocation is magic that involves the summoning of a spiritual being into attendance, usually with the intent of requesting or commanding it to perform some kind of task. This kind of magic has often been artistically portrayed as a magician calling up a spirit, while being protected by a magic circle of some kind. In more modern Pagan religions this act of which craft is usually involves calling spiritual entities to grant protection during rituals. However older occult texts contain great lists of spirit beings like angels that have influence in certain areas and that may be summoned in order to grant assistance in those areas.

Invocation

Invocation is similar to Evocation in that it involves the drawing in of spiritual beings to ones presence. However, when a witch Invokes a being such as a God or Goddess, they call the spiritual being into a host. During this process the mind of the host is to some degree "pushed aside" as the mentality of the spirit being enters the host. This is like a form of willing possession, where the host and spirit merge for a time.

Astral Travel

Spirit Journeys or Astral Travel was often achieved in tribal cultures through many means, including trials of pain and the use of psychedelic herbs. At the height of this experience the magician was said to be able to leave their body and travel in the Astral World (though they wouldn't have called it that), which is synonymous with dreams and spirits. Today this is often called "Astral Projection" and many people perform this through meditative techniques.

Mediumship

This was very popular in Victorian Britain and was often used as a form of entertainment; however the idea of Mediumship has had a very different and magical history across many cultures. Mediumship, in its many different forms, is a way to contact the dead and relay messages from them. In some cases this is done through allowing the deceased to speak through the Medium, but in other cases it is achieved by the Medium acting as an intermediary that interprets and passes along messages from the dead.

Healing

The art of healing has perhaps been the most common form of magic on every continent across the world at some time or another. Whether it be through herbalism, ritual or similar magics, there has always been a need for doctors in some form or another. This duty commonly fell to Priests and similar religious leaders who would work their arts to ensure the health of the community and cure the ailments of individuals. Herb Lore was a common and often essential practice among these wise men and women of the tribes, villages and towns. In this way magic often mixed with medicine. Today healing magic is often performed only for minor illnesses like the common cold, in order to try and necessitate a speedy recovery. However, Healing Spells may also be used in conjunction with modern medical science with the hope of helping it along. But most witches these days are more than happy to put their health in the hands of doctors and surgeons.

Cursing

Casting curses is a direct magical attempt to in some way hinder or harm another person or people. Though many may frown upon this practice and shy away from it, it has been a popular practice and remains an essential part of witchcraft even today. In the past this may simply have been an attempt to try and curse enemies of the tribe, such as rival armies and such. But there is no reasoning why cursing cannot be a lot more personal and in all likelihood it probably always has been for the most part. A form of magic that by all technical account comes under the heading of curses is known commonly as a "Binding". Binding spells can be cast upon another person as a hindrance to them. Many would see this as an affront to free-will, which is why it can be put amongst curses. However, it is well worth noting that although a Binding may be negative in some regards, it can also be intended for positive purposes. Regardless, the fear of curses is one of the big reasons that people came to fear witchcraft over the years. Despite this, cursing is still an integral part of witchcraft that should be known, even if it isn't practised.

Blessing

On the other side of the fence we have Blessings - beneficial magic aimed at helping or protecting people in some way. A Blessing can take many forms over many different magical traditions. In some traditions a child may be blessed at birth in a very simple way, whereas other kinds of blessings could involve elaborate rituals. The idea of blessings is a very constant one that has persisted throughout all world cultures in some form, often becoming traditions or superstitions along the way. The origins of some such superstitions have been lost to time, but their quaint idea has remained. Crossing fingers for good luck, wearing something old, new, borrowed and blue during a wedding, having a Priest bless a house; these are all magical acts in their own rights. A Blessing can be placed upon a great number of things, but will generally be placed upon either a person or a place. A very specific type of Blessing in this fashion would be a **Consecration**, which is when an area (or object) is blessed in some way to mark it as a Sacred Space or object. Modern magic has many ways of performing these beneficial magics, including protective spells, spells for luck and even career help.

Amulets

Charms, amulets and talismans are physical items that become the focus of a spell in order to maintain its magical effect. These days amulets and charms are commonly seen in our treasured superstitions that have been handed down in folklore, such as lucky horse-shoes and similar good-luck charms. But historically an amulet was generally some kind of sign or symbol worn in the form of jewellery or clothing. These symbols could be anything from dedications to the Gods to magical sigils of protection. However, an amulet could just as easily be a gemstone, drawing or statue.

Divination

Divination is a form of magic that seeks to obtain information through indirect means. Divination can effectively be broken down into several groups:

Dowsing: The process of finding a place or object by the deciphered movement of an object.

Prophecy: The method of obtaining information, usually from a divine source.

Fortune-Telling: There are a vast array of methods for fortune telling, from Tarot Cards to Runes, but the intent is always to provide an insight into what the future holds.

Omens: Reading Omens is the practice of deciphering events and signs in the natural world in order to gain insight into either current or future events.

Scrying: Scrying is the method of using a visual focus in order to see over distances or into the future. This could also be said to include viewing into other planes of existence.

Necromancy: Similar to Mediumship, Necromantic Divination is the practice of summoning the dead so that they can divine the future or reveal information.

In some instances a magician may also summon some kind of spirit so that they may perform divination for the magician. Not all forms of divination are necessarily "magic" in the conventional sense, often being more a matter of keen insight or even psychic ability, but at the same time there are a good number of divination methods that can be defined as magic.

Exorcism

Magic for the forcible removal of unwanted spirits is also one of the most common forms of magic in many cultures. A lot of the time this means removing a spirit of some sort when they have possessed a human body against that person's will, but this category can also be said to include **Banishings** which is a common term used in witchcraft and magic for the dismissal or forcible removal of a spirit being from a particular place.

Alchemy

Alchemy is the mystical and magical work of transforming one thing into another. When most people think of alchemy they think of the process of turning lead into gold. While it is true that this is an alchemical process, it is not really the larger intent of alchemy. The "Great Work" of alchemy is about personal transformation, improving the soul and increasing the length & quality of life. This is summarised in what is known as the search for the Philosopher's Stone (nothing to do with Harry Potter). In truth, alchemy probably doesn't belong in this list, but it is included simply because the idea of personal transformation can be a very real objective in magic.

Petitions

This is probably the most practised form of magic in the world and involves asking a divine power to aid you in some way. The most common way to petition the Gods is through prayer, but a person may also use music, sacrifices or other offerings. This is a magical act in the sense that you are attempting to reach out into the greater levels of the universe and contact the Gods, often as part of a larger magical working. Not all petition are magic, but they can be.

It is very likely that when working any kind of magical ritual or spell, the work that is being done will encompass a fair number of these magical varieties. For example, a Wiccan is probably going to be using evocations in the process of creating a Magic Circle, but the Circle itself is Sacred Space, thus Blessed and Consecrated. In addition to these things though, one form of magic that has not been mentioned is "Unweaving" or "Breaking" a spell. Breaking a spell means that a magic act that has been set in motion is interrupted and stopped. Views on how this is achieved and who can do it vary greatly. Many magic users view this as something that the caster themselves cannot do and that they must instead endure the consequences of their spell-working. But it is an equally common view that spells like curses can be broken by another person, while I have also heard it said that only the caster of a spell can break it. Unweaving a magical act is in itself a magical act and has a great wealth of tradition and folklore behind it that differs across different cultures and indeed, a good many of our myths, legends and fairy tales concern this very subject.

In Accordance with Nature

Our universe is conveniently outfitted with certain laws that keep it ticking over quite nicely. Common sense alone would tell us that attempting to do something that messes with these laws is sheer folly. Magic is no different. In magic we recognise that the universe has certain ways and means that it will naturally take in any situation – usually by means of the easiest available option. The magic user learns to behave in the same way, attempting to make her magic work in accordance with the flow of nature for optimum results. This has always been the traditional way to do magic in most cultures. The magic user does not simply cast a spell and then expect to sit back and reap the results. No, magic is more often an accompaniment to action, rather than the action in itself. If a person beseeches a witch for a love spell to make the target of their desire enamoured with them, the witch may cast such a spell but along with the instruction for the seeker to go to the object of their desire so that the spell can be made fruitful. Likewise it is utterly pointless to cast a spell to help you find a better job if you don't actually get up and look for one.

Magic is made to take the easiest course and will become most effective by understanding the flow of the world around you. If our hypothetical love seeker remains too shy to talk to the object of his affections, or our job seeker just sits around watching TV, then a barrier has automatically been placed against the magic, making it much harder for it to achieve its goal. But looking for jobs and at least being in the same place as the other person, creates natural avenues through which the spell can go so that it can achieve the results sought. In days of old, a Priest or Medicine Man may have blessed their tribe so that it would win battles against their enemies, but that didn't mean that the battle would not be fought. Nobody expected the magic to just destroy their enemies without the need of raising a finger. In most cases the magic woven would be to gain the blessings of the Gods of the tribe and to make their warriors strong and skilful in order to win great victory over their enemies.

Nature and Destiny

When considering the flow of nature it is also prudent to consider it in the concept of time and destiny – that which is inevitable. For the sake of this article we will reduce "destiny" to simply mean the things that are sure to happen. In different cultures that would mean different things. Some may see it as the manifest will of the Gods, while others would see it simply as the inevitable results that occur from the things that we do. Cause and effect – Action and reaction. Either way destiny is a real thing. Nobody can argue that the actions we take do not create consequences in our future and that those consequences cause yet more events to spring into action and these lead to further occurrences, and so on and so forth. As the ripples of our actions grow outward from us, they touch the lives of a great many people and the effects can be felt far and wide. The more significant our actions, the further the effects will spread. Destiny, in this sense at least, is an existent thing. The Teutonic people looked upon this as Wyrd, that which must happen due to our actions in the present, while in Hinduism it is called Karma. The magician who is mindful to the passage of time and the way that events in the world will likely take shape, can work their magic along the course of destiny, casting their magics at the most beneficial times and acting in a manner that best allows them to work in accordance with natural destiny.

If you see destiny to be the result of the will of the Gods, then it makes sense that the natural flow of your magic should work best when it is aligned with the will of the Gods – or at least when it is not counter to their will. Of course, this in itself can be problematic, as you are then having to consider exactly which Gods are relevant to your workings. But a common feature in magic is to seek the blessings of the Gods so that the spell is worked with greater power and approval from the divine. In so doing, the magic becomes one with the will of the Gods, rather than a separate occurrence that the Gods may or may not take issue with.

However, there is also another way to look at destiny and that is in the form of your own personal destiny that you are uniquely entitled to strive for. In this instance your destiny becomes the penultimate future that you create for yourself when working in accordance with your true nature and the nature of the universe. This vision of destiny is the realistic utilisation of all your talents, abilities and flaws, allowing you to reach the ultimate achievement that is possible for you in this life. Fulfilling this destiny is being able to completely reach your spiritual, mental, psychological, social and physical peak, and have them all exist together in harmonious union. Each of us has the capability to reach this lofty height and achieve our highest destiny, but not everyone is able to answer this call. Through deep inner searching and a full understanding of who you are, a person can strive towards this destiny, working in accordance with their own natures and the nature of the universe around them. Any magic that is complimentary to this objective and follows the path of this personal destiny is working in accordance with your True Nature, striving to achieve a magical goal that works within the reality of who you are and what you are capable of, while allowing you to build towards your destined self.

The Inner Flow of Nature

When seeking to work in accordance with the natural flow it is very easy to get lost in the outward view of the spell, considering how the spell will best work in accordance with external reality. However it is just as important to understand the workings of your own inner world. Returning again to the words of Aleister Crowley:

"A Man whose conscious will is at odds with his True Will is wasting his strength. He cannot hope to influence his environment effectively."

As has already been noted when discussing magical tools, in magic we establish a link in our psyche between the conscious and the unconscious, as well as the higher aspects of ourselves. Magic is woven by achieving a harmonious unity within ourselves. So if what we are attempting to do is in some way different or against what we really think, feel or believe, then we have automatically created a magical blockade against ourselves casting successful magic. Unity of the internal self cannot be achieved when we are experiencing inner discord. So before even attempting magic, the wise person attempts to understand the real nature of what they are considering and ask the hard questions of themselves. "Is this what I really want?" "Am I willing to deal with the consequences?" "Do I need this?"

All these questions (and more) are important considerations when looking to do magic and it is well worth considering the implications of what these questions are asking.

Firstly, *"Is this what I really want?"*

Obviously this is a key question for many reasons. By asking this we are really giving some proper consideration to who we are and what it is that we want to achieve. By asking this question we explore our own natures, as well as the nature of the magic we are considering. In doing this we need to think about what the benefit of this magic will be and whether that result is in accordance with what we want in every regard. Is it just a passing whim or does it conform with the big picture of your life? If you are planning on working magic, take the time to understand who you are and what you want, so you can tell if the magic in question is really right for you.

Next, *"Am I willing to deal with the consequences?"*

A very important question and even asking it shows that you understand magic comes with big responsibilities. You can't perform any act in your life without there being consequences and this is especially true of magic. It needs to be considered what the actual objective of the magic will bring about and if that is something that you want and can handle. In addition you need to consider what additional consequences will come from this magic. Who else will it affect? How long will it last? Is it morally right to you? When weighing up all the consequences, can you live with them?

When considering consequences, it is also worth keeping in mind that magic is very often unpredictable. You may know what you want and then structure your magic to achieve that goal, but the way the magic achieves it isn't always the way we may have envisions. I've heard many tales from a variety of magic users about spells that didn't work out the way they expected, or indeed, spells that worked *too* well. This highlights the old saying "be careful what you wish for". So before you do magic, just bare in mind that it may just work in a way you may not expect or want. For this reason, be sure it is worth it.

Finally, *"Do I need this?"*

This question is perhaps more significant than you may think. Our "needs" as a species are actually rather simple and nature does pretty well in providing for these basic needs in most cases and with a little work we can keep these needs appeased without ever having to use magic. But as beings of higher intelligence we also have other *needs* which we consider to be beneficial to our happiness. The question here is do you really require magic in order to gather these things to you and how many of these things do you really need for life and happiness. If what you seek truly is a need, then you are following the flow of your own nature. But be aware that sometimes the things that we think bring us happiness are really just psychological crutches, distractions from our problems and comfortable conveniences. Wisdom is in knowing the difference between the things that really make you happy and the things that you *think* make you happy.

If you can justify the magic with your True Will, then you have set the stage for creating inner harmony and projecting your magic into the rest of the universe with the strength of your entire being.

A Life of Magic

I have often encountered people seeking magical aids to their life as a way to deal with certain problems and circumstances. But sometimes we need to consider the benefit of **not** doing magic. Life is made up of good times and bad, and they are both just as valuable as each other. We need the good and the bad times in order to be well rounded people and in order to be better people, both spiritually and psychologically. Life isn't candy-coated; it can be harsh and painful at times. Magic is not a way to avoid this and (in the opinion of this author) it shouldn't be used as such. Life certainly can be harsh, but it can also be wonderful and joyous. It is important for us to understand and experience both sides of this so that we can grow, but it is also important to experience each in order to recognise them for what they are. We only know pleasure because we can compare it to pain and we only understand what joy is because we can compare it to sadness. Good and bad compliment each other.

Magic is not a solution to life; it is an accompaniment to it.

The intention should never be to use magic as a way to avoid living. Life is both good and bad, if you try to cut out all the unpleasant bits with magic, then you aren't only attempting to move against the nature of life itself, you are also attempting to only live half a life. Life has many lessons to teach us and some of them are best learnt through the bad times. Do yourself the honour of allowing you the opportunity to live life in the best possible way. Learn from the hard times, enjoy the good times and face them both with dignity and strength. Magic is just a tool, a craft; it is not a replacement for living.

Pagan Generation

Pagan Rituals

Ritual is belief in action. It is taking theory, idea and spiritual commitment, and moving them into the realm of being. Through ritual we express our beliefs and give them life.

Rituals serve all manner of purposes, from the mundane to the magical, but ultimately they serve to express what is within us; to give us an outlet for our spirituality that reveals not only what we believe, but also what those beliefs mean in grand scope of the universe.

While it is true that a ritual can be said to imply any kind of repetitive task, this article is about Pagan Ritual and the religions that use them. So we will be focusing on rituals and magical workings in this regard, providing an insight into what they mean and how to construct your own.

Rituals

Every religion in the world has it's rituals of one kind or another and for this reason it would become impractical to even try and list them all here. For this reason I would suggest that you take the time to look into the rituals that are closest to your religious beliefs or otherwise connected to the Gods that you revere. However, this article isn't primarily about rituals that already exist, it is about creating your own. Obviously those that are already out there are well worth looking into. If nothing else they can provide great examples that can feed your imagination when creating your own. But on the subject of rituals, I feel it is beneficial to take a brief look at a summary of different *types* of ritual, in order to create a grounding that we can build into.

Types of Ritual

Honouring/Worship

Among the most common rituals are those used to give reverence to someone or something. This most often means a God or Gods, but can also include ancestors, spirit beings, faeries, dragons or even a certain person within the community, such as a great leader or spiritual advisor. The key goal in rituals of this sort is that they aim to offer praise and respect to a certain person, people or beings. In most incidents this would involve that individual(s) to be present to receive that honouring, so in the case of Gods and spirits, this often involves summoning them to attendance or holding the ritual in a place sacred to those that are being honoured, such as a temple or sacred grove. Worship in these rituals can be offered in many ways, including sacrifices, offerings, prayer, song and possibly even poetic verse.

Marriage

Wedding ceremonies extend across just about every culture in some way and exist in many forms in different mythologies. Even the Gods get married in myth, with great celebrations to mark the event (often coupled by some rather extreme honeymoons). Marriages aren't always seen to be involving the Gods; sometimes they are merely declarations of a loving union between those involved. However, more often these unions are symbolised by elaborate rituals that are both social and spiritual events for those involved, with the Gods in witness of the union.

Funerary

People die and worldwide humanity has come to commemorate their passing. Strangely, rites and rituals to mark death are probably more common around the world than those to mark birth. The commonality between all funerary rites is in some predetermined disposal of the body, either in burial, entombment, burning or mummification. But the rituals themselves that precede or follow this are often intended to mark the life of the individual and help them to cross into the other world with ease. Sometimes the Gods or another spiritual being will be called upon to receive the soul of the deceased and escort them into their next life.

Seasonal

Most of our yearly rituals take place on the same date each year. But some there are some rituals that exist to mark a seasonal event in itself. Ancient Celtic and modern neo-Pagan religions (among others) have many rituals to celebrate the passing of the seasons and these are often envisioned in the lives of the Gods. The Season holidays of modern Paganism are probably the most well known events that those new to Paganism will encounter first. They will also seem the most familiar, as a large number of them were co-opted by Christianity and have become our more well-known holidays in the West.

Revelry

Sometimes a party just doesn't need any other reason. Some religions have rituals that exist for no other reason than to celebrate, raise energy and lift the spirits of the group. These celebrations are often a part of some particular religious event, like honouring a certain God, but in these cases it seems those Gods are honoured by just having the best time that you can have. A good example of these would be the public festivals dedicated to Gods such as Dionysus, which involved several days of partying, drinking and merriment. Or across Europe from our Nordic brethren we have rituals such as the Sumbel, which is a traditional drinking celebration. This celebration can contain many ritual acts, including toasting the Gods, celebrating your past, present and future, and tale-spinning. In some cases these revelries also serve a dual purpose, such as receiving prophetic visions through drinking and ecstatic dance, as may have been the practice in the ancient Mystery Religions, or setting in motion the events that we desire for the future by declaring them at the toast of a drink before your gathered friends.

Atonement

Rituals of atonement are pledges of apology and requests for forgiveness. These kinds of rituals are probably less common in Paganism; however the idea of reclaiming ones own honour and dignity through deeds certainly isn't, as is depicted in the literature surrounding our Pagan ancestors. In many ways this outlines a crucial difference between Pagan religions and Abrahamic religions, as Paganism very often prefers the idea of making up for the mistakes you make, as opposed to simply confessing them. However, that being said, there are still examples (mostly in folklore or myth) of people making offering and sacrifices to the Gods and other beings in order to atone for some mistake they have made. But mythology also implies that Pagan Gods don't always take kindly to being offended; often conjuring up some rather imaginative punishments for those that offend them the most.

Play Acting

Rituals of this type are probably among the most fun, at least for those who like to take centre stage. In these rituals, those gathered assume the roles of certain figures (usually mythological) and either through a script or through improvisation, they act out a scene or story that is related to those characters. These rituals are to celebrate those being imitated and to directly show the lessons that their tales teach us. These days rituals of this kind aren't all that common, but in some form they can occasionally be found in modern practices, but usually without such a focused structure. The one that you will probably be most familiar with is the Nativity play, though this isn't Pagan, but similar play acting is also used by Masons and to some degree, Wiccans (among others). However, just because it isn't all that common doesn't mean that you shouldn't use play acting yourself, assuming you can get others to share your act.

Purification

Purification rituals are fairly common in Paganism, especially tribal based religions. Rituals like this can be utilised with the intent of purifying the body, mind and soul. They tend to act as a way to focus the will of the individual and in some way make them better, cleaner and worthy of taking part in other things. A ritual of purification you may be aware of is a baptism, where a person symbolically cleans themselves of sin so that they may continue in the religion. However, in Paganism baptisms can be performed using any element, especially water and fire. But Purification rituals needn't be focused on a person, they can also be performed on a place in the form of a Consecration. In doing this a location is cleansed in the same way, often for the sake of performing other rituals work there. Consecrated ground is generally considered to be Sacred Space, such as ritual circles, burial mounds or sacred groves.

Anointing

Similar to purification rituals, but with a different intent. Where purification is used to rid a person of some kind of negative element about themselves, an Anointment is a way to prepare a person for a larger working. When anointed the individual is made ready to receive a connection to the larger powers of the universe, having been marked as worthy of this kind of connection. In this way it is a focus for the mind and spirit of the person, allowing them to enter into the ritual mindset that they will need in order to connect to the spiritual energies around them.

Rites of Passage

There are a great many Rites of Passage in life and our many world cultures have made some exceptional rituals to celebrate them. A rite of passage is designed to mark the passing from one point in life, into another of notable significance. This could be the passage into adulthood, an initiation into a group, the marked onset of old age, a personal Dedication ritual, or the ascension to a certain position of prestige.

Constructing a Ritual

With a good idea of what you believe and the path that you wish to follow, you can begin to construct rituals in accordance to your beliefs. If you are lucky then you will already have some idea as to the kind of rituals that are practised in your religion. If so then this step by step guide will act as a source to help you put your beliefs into action.

Step One
What do I want to do?

This is the most obvious first consideration. There is no point in even considering a ritual if you haven't a clue of what it is that you are trying to achieve. Look into the beliefs of your religion and use the examples above as a way to steer you onto the kind of thing that you wish to do. Remember, entering into a ritual practice is not just a dull repetition of words and actions that you have written down in advance, it is an expression of your inner self, as such, ritual is a way to adjust your mindset and use the practice to not only impact your own psychology, but also a way to leave a lasting mark on the spiritual environment around you. If any ritual is done correctly, then the person or people doing it will be putting their energies, thoughts and feelings into the ritual, speaking from their heart and attempting to really make it mean something. Because of this, a successful ritual can't help but leave an impression upon the surrounding spiritual landscape, even if only for a short time. This is important to consider, because if you are going to apply that much of yourself into something then you should really understand what it is you are doing and perhaps more importantly, why you are doing it. If, however, you are not putting your whole heart into the ritual, then is there really any point in doing it? So when asking yourself what you want to do in your ritual, remember to consider what that means. Once you understand that, you will have the groundwork for where the rest of your ritual is heading.

Step Two
Where shall I hold my Ritual?

Among many Pagan traditions there is a practice in which the place that you hold a ritual should either have sacred significance, or otherwise be prepared as sacred space for the purpose of the ritual. For our ancestors this may have involved worshipping in sacred groves or maybe amongst the standing stones across Europe. But these days such things aren't too easy to come buy. While it is true that you can feel free to practice in a woodland clearing that provides you with a sense of spiritual significance, it is often far more practical to simply set aside some easily accessible space and sanctify it. In modern witchcraft, this practice is usually achieved through sweeping an area to rid it of negative energies and then casting a Magic Circle. Ceremonial Magicians, on the other hand, tend to set aside some space in their home to use as a permanent temple or sacred space. For some of us this isn't a practical option and so a temporary temple can be made that may be quickly erected when needed.

We'll discuss how to create Sacred Space shortly.

Step Three
When should I perform it?

Rituals are generally held in order to mark an event of some sort, so of course it makes sense to perform your ritual to coincide with the event you are marking. Seasonal Rituals are perhaps the most obvious examples, held in order to mark the significance of the changing seasons or some other celestial event. For rituals with a little more flexibility, there are other aspects that you may want to consider when determining the timing of your ritual. Some examples may be the day of the week, the position of the Moon (or other planets) and the time of day or night. Considering these kinds of things can also be useful for magical works, so if you intend on working magic in your ritual, it may be a good idea to take timing into account for that reason.

Moon phases

Different phases of the Moon are said to be appropriate times for different kind of workings. For example, in some traditions of Wicca, monthly Esbats would ideally be held on the Full Moon. But the Moon can play a part in the timing of a ritual in other ways, too.

> **New Moon:** The Dark Moon, invisible to the eye, is a time of preparation. The Moon is yet to be reborn, so rituals and magic concerning new beginnings are best performed at this time. In some traditions this time is seen as a time of rest when no magics are worked, but in others it may be looked upon as a good time for beginning new ventures. Perhaps if you were planning some kind of Dedication Ritual, this would be the best time, as it is a for examination of hidden things and mysteries, as well as new beginnings.
>
> **Waxing Moon:** When the moon becomes visible again and is in a state of growth, this is known as its "waxing" time. Workings that focus on growth and development may be best suited to this time, but as such it can also be a time for improvement in situations of love and general blessings, with the idea that as the moon grows, so too will the strength of the blessing. At this phase in the Moon's cycle, it is manifest once more

and so it is a good time to do rituals and magic, which are geared towards bringing something into being or drawing things close to you.

Full Moon: The Moon is full and pregnant now, bursting with light and power. This time is good for a great many workings, especially those concerning female and Goddess energies. The cycle of the Moon can be compared to female menstrual cycle and at this time it is at the height of its majesty. This makes it a good time for fertility rites and calling upon female deities. In addition, because the moon is at the fullest point in its cycle, it is a good time to focus on culminations and the fruition of any other things you have been working towards. This is when the energies of the pregnant moon are ready to help all your plans peak and deliver the greatest bounty. The Full Moon has long had a reputation for affecting people's minds, causing a temporary lunacy. Perhaps this is why the Full Moon is often seen as a good time for revelry and merriment. Many also see the Full Moon as appropriate for the exploration of their psychic potential and the development of that part of themselves.

Waning Moon: As the moon shrinks and recedes back into darkness, it symbolises a movement towards death. Because of this it is a good time to perform magics and rituals that focus upon endings. This is a time of destruction, as the moon starts to disappear again, so workings in that theme are well placed now. Stopping unwanted habits, breaking curses and ending relationships are good examples of workings for this time. It can also be a time to rest and take a break from things. Some may see this as a good time for contacting the dead, but others would consider such things better suited to either the Full Moon or New Moon.

Days of the Week

The days of the week are seen as significant in many ways. Firstly, the days themselves are names after certain Gods and so if working with these Gods that might be a good time to petition them. Otherwise, the days also have other correspondences.

Monday: The day of the Moon. Thus it is good for work that involves female issues, emotions and the Mysteries. Unsurprisingly, this day is ruled by the Moon.

Tuesday: Tyr's Day. Tyr was a Norse God, noted for his great valour in combat and his incredible honesty. He was willing to sacrifice his hand so that the Gods could bind the great wolf Fenrir. The Romans marked this day by the God Mars, who is still the planet associated with Tuesday. Workings for this day have definitely picked up the traits of Tyr and Mars, as today is regarded as a good time for works of discipline, courage, athletics and passion.

Wednesday: Odin's Day (Woden's Day). Odin was the All Father, chief among the Norse Gods. He was seen to be the wisest of the Gods and tore out his own eye so that he might obtain the secrets of the Runes, which were later gifted to mankind. Wednesday is ruled by the planet Mercury, who also shares some connection to the naming of the day from the Latin. This day has attained correspondences with both Odin and Mercury. It is seen as seen as a good day for workings regarding wisdom and artistic pursuits, but also communication and travel.

Thursday: Thor's Day. Thor was a God of Thunder and struck down his enemies using the magical hammer, Mjolnir. Thursday was attributed to Jupiter by the Romans. Jupiter, as an equivalent to Thor in the naming of the day, also wielded the power of the thunderbolt. The alignment of this day has kept more in connection to Jupiter (which is its ruling planet), than it has to Thor. Thusly this day is good for workings that focus on leadership, prosperity, wealth and health.

Friday: Frigg's Day. Frigg is the wife of Odin and a Goddess associated with love, marriage, fertility and motherhood. It is no surprise then that she should become the equivalent to Venus who marked this day for the Romans. Venus is still the ruling planet of this day, which is why this day is best used for workings of love, romance, friendship, sex and beauty.

Saturday: Saturn's Day. This is the only day that has retained a directly Roman name, in their God Saturn. Saturn was the God of the harvest and so this day can be seen to be a time to reap rewards of labour and to put an end to work for a time. Pretty appropriate for the start of the weekend, really. However, Saturn is comparable also to the Greek God Cronus, the ruler of the Golden Age of man. Cronus' mythology shows him as a conqueror who attempts to gain and maintain his power. This day mirrors that to a degree, as it is seen as good time for workings that involve removing obstacles and addressing problems.

Sunday: The Day of the Sun. Of course this day is rather unsurprisingly aligned with the Sun. As the Sun is the ruler of the sky, today is a day for authority, success and sovereignty. Preceding the feminine alignment of

Monday, Sunday has masculine connections and so is a good time for performing workings that relate to men.

Night and Day

To some, the different hours of the day hold different astrological connections. However, listing these out as well could take up a severe amount of space that just isn't constructive to this article, so instead we'll look at the basic principles of Night and Day.

Day time: As the Sun is in the sky, this is obviously the best time for any kind of working that relates to the Sun. But that doesn't mean that it is the only time when you can work with these energies. The daytime is light and exposed, so it is a good time for open celebrations, especially those that you don't mind being public. As a very male orientated time it is well disposed for celebrations of virility and athletic activities. The Sun is also very significant for Solstice and Equinox rituals, in which the entire point is to use the passage of the Sun as the ritual focus, marking the shortest and longest days of the year, as the Sun enters its lowest and highest phases.

Night time: Night is for private functions and secret gatherings. As a time of darkness it is closely connected to the Mysteries, so it is well suited to these kinds of rituals. The Moon is the ruler of the night, serving as the light in the darkness. As mentioned, the moon is aligned to feminine energies and so the night is well disposed to working with feminine energies. But there is no reason you shouldn't work with these energies at other times, too. The night also reveals to us the constellations of the stars and so it is a good time for considering other astrological works.

One may wish to take into account other aspects of timing, such as astrological alignments and mystical numerology. If these things interest you at all then I would recommend looking into books on these subjects or otherwise checking the internet. Various paths may place different significance to different numbers, times and heavenly events, so to make things easier, first look to see if your specific religion/path has any teachings regarding these things.

Step Four
What do I need?

Preparation really is the key to any successful ritual. Really, there is no worse situation to be in than to reach a crucial moment in a ritual only to discover you have left something important in your kitchen or forgotten to prepare appropriate words for that part.

Preparing a ritual is in itself a very significant part of the entire process, not only for the obvious need to know what you are going to do, but also because in the preparation of a ritual you are forced to give some thought into what each and every step in that ritual signifies and consider why you will be performing each bit. For the solo practitioner this gives a situation where there shouldn't be anything in the ritual that doesn't hold some kind of personal significance, while for the group based ritual the members have the opportunity to attain an understanding of a ritual from many different perspectives and even learn about new things in context to the ritual. This stage is the opportunity to learn and expand your understanding of what you are doing, so feel free to take your time and really put your mind into your ritual.

Scripting

The best way to prepare your ritual is to write it down, planning it step by step on paper so that you can get a real impression of how it is going to run and everything you will be doing. Treat your ritual like a script, complete with dialogue and stage directions. Learn it as best you can so that your ritual goes smoothly.

Scripting out your ritual also provides you with the additional benefit of giving you a hard copy that outlines everything else you will need for your ritual. Go through it and use it as a way to make a list of all the tools, ingredients and similar items that you will need, so that you can get them all gathered together ready before you begin.

Tools

Having taken the time to script out your ritual, you should already be aware of what tools you will need in order to perform it. But more importantly, you should have had an opportunity to examine their significance.

In rituals we use a great many tools that serve a variety of purposes. Some tools are purely practical, while others are used because of what they signify. Common examples of these kinds of tools are as follows:

Effigies

An effigy is a small statue or image and in rituals they are often used to represent different Gods. When used, an effigy can be a focus for prayers, petitions or the attendance of a deity. Effigies show how that figure is deemed to be important and may even be thought of as presiding over the ritual. Instead of effigies some people will simply use lit candles to represent their deities and this is absolutely fine. If you feel this is more appropriate for you, then by all means do so. It is important to understand that when effigies are used, they are not offered any kind of worship themselves. No, the effigy is merely a representation of that God or Goddess and any worship offered is to the actual deity and not the statue.

Censers, Incense and Offerings

If your ritual is intended to give worship then it may be appropriate to make some kind of offering or sacrifice. Incense is a common offering in many religions, with certain scents thought of as being pleasing to the Gods. If you intend on doing this then you will need to make sure you have the appropriate incense, as well as a burner or censer with which to use it. The smoke from incense can also be used to represent the element of Air or for some it may be used to help purify an area. However, some people simply find that incense just makes for a more pleasant environment in which to work.

Altar

An altar is like the workbench of a ritual. Although not all rituals will use altars, those that do may use them a great variety of ways. Generally speaking, a ritual that uses an altar revolves around the altar. That is, the altar makes up a very central point of the ritual, if not for symbolic reason, then for sheer practical reasons of having a place to put all other tools. An altar may serve as a place to keep tools, make offerings and direct the ritual from.

Magical Tools as Ritual tools

The same tools that may be used in magical acts often all serve as ritual tools, as well. Blades, drinking vessels, wands, etc. can and do serve purposes beyond the magical. Some may serve to indicate who is leading a ritual or who is responsible for certain tasks, while others can have their own distinct ritual uses. Examine the tools of your path and see if any of them are appropriate to your ritual.

Seasonal Adornments

In rituals designed to mark certain seasonal celebrations, there are often a variety of decorations that are added to houses and ritual spaces in order to add to the festivities. Tinsel, Jack O'Lanterns, holly and mistletoe are good examples of season adornments that can be added to a ritual and in some cases putting up these decorations can be a ritual in and of itself.

Practical Tools

Along with magical and ritual tools, you have to consider the practical things you will need, such as torches for finding your way to outdoor rituals, candle holders and rubbish bags. It's the practical tools that can catch a lot of people out the first time round. Need to light candles? Make sure you have a lighter or matches. Need to cut food? Make sure you have a knife. Will you be drinking in your ritual? Be sure to bring cups. It's the little things like this that can turn an otherwise well planned ritual into chaos and disorder.

Ingredients

You might like to consider certain ingestible ingredients for your ritual, such as drink, cakes or bread. Indeed, some rituals revolve around the idea of consuming food and drink, or otherwise have an official meal that takes place after the main ritual itself. Alternatively, you may need to consider ingredients in regards to spell components, if you are intending on working magic during a ritual.

Attire

Ritual dress can be a big part of any working. Robes, cords and jewellery help you to get in the right frame of mind, as well as signifying that the ritual is something special that deserves its own proper dress. In addition, some items of clothing can be symbolic in their own right, both for the individual wearing them and for use in the actual ritual. Ritual dress can also mean costumes used for play acting, which can be anything from crowns and animals skins, to full on character regalia.

Magic in Rituals

You may wish to perform magic during a ritual and this is completely fine. Indeed, some rituals have no purpose beyond working magic. The only real consideration to take into account when wanting to work magic as part of a ritual is whether or not the magic you are considering is appropriate to the rest of the ritual that is taking place. After all, a spell designed to help you quit smoking wouldn't really sit too well within a ritual designed to celebrate the birth of a God.

Performing magics within a ritual when the two are not compatible to each other can undermine both the ritual and the magic you are trying to create. One brings forth one mindset while the other would require a sudden shift into another desire and mentality. Basically, when you create your ritual space, you do so with an intent and it is best to stay within the alignment of that intent.

Indeed, your mentality is something that is worth keeping in mind with regard to rituals and magic, and a good reason not to overdo the use of spell work in a ceremony. But then there are also the practical implications of having more to remember and the problems with space on your altar. Your ritual space will only be so big and trying to do lots of spells all at once will just create clutter, both mentally and physically in your ritual space.

However, there is no reason why you can't work magics as part of a ritual even if you have no singular intention for it. Lots of groups use rituals as an opportunity to raise power within their circle and then direct it out into the universe with nothing more than "positive intent".

Spell Craft

Spells in themselves often take the shape of rituals in their own right. As such they can be designed along similar guidelines, although there may be more things to consider in regards to how, when and why you are casting the spell. But as far as designing your spells goes, it is also worth thinking about how your magical methods will fit into the rituals you are already doing. Consider if you will need extra tools for your spell or whether you will require additional items. If you do need additional items, will you be able to easily make space for them in your ritual space?

Perhaps more importantly though, is the method you will use to weave your spell. Some methods may not be practical in your ritual space, such as drumming and dancing, which could require more space than you have and possibly annoy your neighbours if you will be working inside. So be sure to consider the hidden variables when designing your spells working.

An example of an Honouring Ritual

Here is an example for a Ritual layout which you can use as a guide to creating your own similar rituals. This ritual is designed for honouring the Gods, but also includes the use of basic magic. However, this simple layout can be adapted for a great variety of rituals. Feel free to experiment and find what is best for you.

Before You Begin
Before you begin your ritual it is common to take time cleaning your tools, the ritual space and cleaning yourself. Much of the time this is a method for focusing your mind towards the work you are soon to engage in.

Cleaning Tools: Spending time in silence cleaning your tools is a way to focus your mind as a method of meditation. As you sit cleaning your ritual tools you rest your mind upon them, contemplating what they are and how they are about to be used. You will consider their symbolism and reaffirm your connection to these items, charging them with your own energies as you clean them.

Bathing: Ritual bathing can be a significant part of preparing for your ritual. It allows you to not only clean yourself (preferable for skyclad rituals), but also to "cleanse" your mind of distractions. This is like a small purification ritual before moving into your larger working.

Cleaning the Ritual Space: Sweeping, anointing and preparing the space for your ritual is in itself a significant act. It announces that something special is about to take place there and that the area is being made suitable for it. This cleansing is not just for brushing away dust and dirt, though, it is more about ridding the area of any energies that may be unwanted in the space of the ritual.

Preparing the Altar
The altar is the work-space of a ritual and the usually the central point of the ritual's Sacred Space. As the focal point of the ritual, the altar becomes the place the gives your ritual direction, as it is a place to keep your ritual tools, ingredients and any offering that you may be using.

Depending upon your tradition, the placement of your altar may be significant. It has become common custom in many groups to place the altar facing North, however some people may find more significance in having a South facing altar. Others may change the position of their altar depending on the rite that is being performed.

> **North:** North is customary to some Traditions as it was seen as the home of the Gods and so any altar that is facing North is automatically aligned towards the Gods and ready to worship them.
>
> **East:** The East is the point from which the Sun rises every day and so a lot of Traditions place their altar facing East and begin their rituals in that quarter, as the origin of light and revelation.
>
> **South:** The South is the high-point of the sun, associated with passion and energy. Not many Traditions place their altar in the South, but some groups may choose this position for certain rituals.
>
> **West:** Altars in the West are suited to workings of deep emotion and the subconscious. The sun sets in the West and as the place of darkness it is associated with the Mysteries.

When preparing your altar, make sure that you have placed upon it or around it, all items that you will need for your ritual, including any tools, effigies and seasonal adornments.

Creating Sacred Space

Sacred space is the difference between somewhere that you *could* hold a ritual and somewhere that is worthy of your ritual. The term "Sacred Space" can mean many things to may people and the methods for creating it can vary from tradition to tradition. Some religions will have temples or churches that are built and are sacred spaces unto themselves, and some Pagans will similarly have a temple set up in their house, if they are lucky. But for many Pagans the matter of creating Sacred Space involves doing so each time they hold a ritual.

Sacred Space is basically taking the area of your ritual and before you begin, marking it in some way in order to consecrate it to your purpose. This can be a simple symbolic act, perhaps involving a small dedication to the Gods, or it can be a significant part of the ritual itself, in which surrounding and personal energies are drawn together in order to align the space to your working.

The act of creating Sacred Space is common to a good majority of Pagan paths and they all have their own ways of doing it, which despite appearing different in their methods, remain extremely similar in their theory and intent. Here are a few examples:

> **Heathenry:** A common method in Asatru for creating Sacred Space before a ritual is called "The Hammer Rite". This rite is a Neo-Pagan development, but believed by many to be based around the symbolism of Mjollnir, the hammer of Thor. This rite usually involves a dual declaration, one towards the altar and one facing away from it (covering both directions of the ritual space), in which the person calls upon the hammer to sanctify the space. This is sometimes coupled with the striking of a hammer in each direction.
>
> **Kemeticism:** In the Kemetic religion, the Sacred Space is created by purifying the Shrine (akin to the altar, here). This is done by physically cleaning the Shrine and the area around it and then touching each object on the Shrine with a mixture of water and Natron. Natron is a substance natural to Egypt, but can be (effectively) made at home by combining baking soda and salt. As the objects are touched and cleansed, the Kemetic concentrates on making the area a place that is suitable for the Gods to visit.
>
> **Wicca:** Ritual Sacred Space is created in Wicca through the casting of a Magic Circle. This is done by magically drawing in the energies that naturally surround the caster and projecting them into a protective circle. The area within this Circle will be the Sacred Space of the ritual. In addition to this, Wiccans call upon the services of supernatural beings of the Elements to act as guardians and observers at the four cardinal points of the Circle; North, East, South and West. The building of the Circle is very much a ritual unto itself and as such forms a significant part of the greater ritual workings that will take place within it.

When we create Sacred Space we are seen to do so on multiple levels, cleansing the area on the physical plane and on the spiritual plane, while also clearing our own minds so that we may be better disposed towards what we are about to do. It is an act of purification and consecration, making the area worthy of our ritual and aligned towards it, while simultaneously doing the same to ourselves.

Opening Your Ritual

With your altar prepared and your Sacred Space cast, it is now time to begin your ritual. As this is a ritual to honour the Gods, it is necessary to begin by declaring to whom you are dedicating the ritual and inviting them to attend. After all, there is no point in throwing a party for someone if you don't invite them along. This part of the ritual is a statement of why you are holding the ritual and a formal request for the guest of honour to join you in the Sacred Space that you have prepared. Once you have called to your God or Goddess (or both), it may be appropriate to officially mark their attendance; perhaps by lighting a candle in their honour. If you are lucky enough to own one, you may want to sound the formal opening of the ritual with the blowing of a Ritual Horn.

The Honouring

Now you have the attendance (or at least the attention) of your desired deity, it is time to really begin the Honouring itself. A statement of recognition is a good way to start, declaring the way in which you personally understand that deity, who they are and what they do. This could be followed with a respectable talk of your own relationship with that deity and what they mean to you.

After this it is a good time to give thanks, letting the God or Goddess in question, know what you are grateful for and what you would like to personally thank them for. What has their presence in your life brought to you? How has your life changed thanks to them? What do they do that you most respect and admire?

An Offering

Honouring your deity needn't be restricted to a simple verbal declaration. This is a chance to really express your honour for you deity in the best way that you can. Feel free to give offerings to your God or Goddess, perhaps in the form of food or incense. For those offering food, it can sometimes be a question as to what you should do with the food. Well, that may very well depend on the God that you are worshipping. If you are honouring a God that is notably charitable and gives high regard to acts of kindness, then perhaps you could gather together the food after the ritual and take it down to a local homeless shelter or otherwise donate it to those more in need of it (unopened, of course). Alternatively, the food can be consumed by you after the ritual is over, with the spiritual essence of the food having been offered up, you can now feast of its worldly essence. On the other hand, if you are performing your ritual outdoors, you could simply leave it there (but don't litter) and no doubt animals will make lunch of it before the day is done (or possibly someone else…).

But your offering needn't be restricted to things like food and drink. This is, after all, supposed to be a personal declaration, so feel free to make it personal. Your offering could be a piece of artwork, a dance, a song, flowers or anything else that you consider appropriate. Reflect upon the mythology of your God or Goddess to understand the kind of things that they like and give them something that would be appreciated. But also reflect upon your own talents so that you can offer something that truly forms a closer connection between you and your deity.

Make it special.

Spell Working

When the main part of your ritual is done, use this time to perform any spell workings that you have worked out in advance. If you have used dance or song to honour your God, then you may want to also use this as a way to build a Cone of Power to empower your magic. This way, the magic that you perform is in keeping with the way in which the rest of the ritual has been held and it can even be used to seek the blessings of your chosen God when it comes to work your magic.

Give thanks and close the ritual

When you are done thank your deity for coming and announce the end of your ritual. This needn't be too long-winded and can quite easily be summed up in a sentence or two, maybe with the ring of a bell or beat of a drum to signify that the ritual is complete.

Finally, dismiss any other attendees such as ancestors and others spirits, if they were invited to attend and if you cast a Magic Circle, be sure to close it.

After Your Ritual

Once your ritual is finished, there are still things to do. If you work with a permanent ritual space, be sure to tidy it up after your ritual. There is no reason to get into bad habits. The altar has a strong connection to your spiritual subconscious, so if you get into the habit of keeping it cluttered and messy, then it is a mark to your personal discipline and will begin to reflect on your attitude and focus in future rituals. In short, stop bad habits before they begin. If you are going to try and maintain a permanent altar, then you should do it properly.

If you have performed your ritual outdoors, then make sure that you have properly cleaned up after yourself! It can be lovely to enact a ritual in a beautiful woodland clearing, but just make sure that you leave it just as beautiful as you found it. Take all litter, ritual bits and personal belongings away with you.

Any temporary altars should be dismantled and cleared away, making especially sure that all candles are extinguished and that no incense has been left burning. Your ritual tools should be cleaned and returned to a safe and special place, as well.

Grounding

After a ritual it is a good idea to Ground yourself, especially if magic has been worked during that ritual. Grounding a method by which we allow the energies f the ritual to drain away and leave us, so that we are not affected by them after the ritual. Grounding also allows us to replenish our own energies by removing our mental focus away from the ritual and into a regular mode of thinking. This way we do not continue to expend our energies haphazardly through unintentional acts of thought. Instead we can replenish our reserves by taking in new energies to replace those we have already spent, drawing them from food, drink and the Earth beneath us.

The process of clearing away and cleaning on the other end of the ritual can act as a good way to ground you. It brings you slowly out of your ritual mindset and allows you move your thoughts towards mentally establishing that the ritual is over and it is time to move on.

Many Traditions enjoy a good meal after a ritual in order to help ground them. This refreshes their minds, fills their bellies and replaces lost energies from the ritual or spell work.

A Grounding Meditation

If you feel like you need to, you can do a short meditation to Ground yourself as well. This short meditation is simply to do and doesn't take long at all. I would also recommend ending it with a nice drink and some food.

> Sit cross legged on the floor, as close to the ground as possible and close your eyes. Feel your bottom against the ground and visualise how your spine curves in at the end, like a tail. Picture this tail taking root in the ground beneath you, slowly digging downwards like the roots of a plant, connecting you to the Earth.

> Imagine that your root is going deep into the Earth and then when it is firmly rooted down, that natural curve takes a hold, securing you there. You are now part of the Earth. You are one with the Earth and its energies and your root will act like a plant, taking in the energies of the Earth and feeding them back up to you.

Imagine these energies filling you up, let them replenish you.

Once you feel refreshes and ready, simply pull back your roots and sit for a moment. Get comfortable and let yourself feel healthier and fuller. You are refreshed and ground. Open your eyes, stand, stretch and have a nice drink.

Wicca: The Old Religion

Wicca is one of the most popular religions in the world today, with an ever increasing interest amongst young and old alike. But what exactly is the Wicca? Wicca is the religion of witchcraft, using magic to weave its rites and honour its deities. Here we will take a look at the Wicca, where it came from and what it means to be a follower of its ways.

What is Wicca?

Wicca is a lot of things all at once. It is a nature religion, a mystery religion, a fertility religion and also a witchcraft tradition. It's all these things rolled together that make it unique. As a nature religion, Wicca respects and reveres the natural world, taking a lot of inspiration from the passage of the seasons and the intricate beauty that is present in the world around us. These natural cycles and occurrences are seen as the interplay of the religion's deities, often referred to as "the God and Goddess".

As a mystery religion, Wicca is a secret to those who don't follow its ways. There is a long standing practice of initiation, through which people interested in the religion and that choose to follow it, may enter into a coven and learn the secret teachings of the Wiccan way. Luckily for us, however, Wiccans have allowed a small glimpse into their world. Many Wiccans have published books on Wicca that help us to understand some of it, or at least enough of it that we can get an idea as to what it is about. But of course, if you wish to know more, then you will need to find a Wiccan coven to teach you.

Wicca is also a fertility religion, placing a lot of emphasis on sex as a sacred practice. This is one reason why the vast majority of Wiccans aren't brought into the religion until they are at least eighteen. However, there is nothing to stop younger people from exploring the religion until then and finding out if it really for them. But fertility also regards the fertility of the land, as well as people, and acknowledges the process and richness of life in its creative process, whether that is in plants, animals or ourselves.

As a witchcraft religion, Wicca utilises magic in its workings. Indeed, witchcraft is a part of Wicca's most fundamental rituals and practices. Through magic, the witches of the Wicca connect to the other aspects of our reality and use the energies around us to work their ways.

Where did it come from?

Wicca is sometimes affectionately known as "The Old Religion", but in actuality it isn't all that old. Wicca was created in the late 1930's to 1940's by a man named Gerald Gardner, but it didn't enter into public knowledge until 1951, when the laws of the Witchcraft Act were repealed in Britain. Gerald Gardner created Wicca using elements of other occult systems and the ideas of older Pagan religions, though he also claimed he himself was initiated into a coven of witches and that the beliefs of his Wicca were based on their teachings.

So why do people call it The Old Religion?

Well, even though Wicca isn't actually that old, it does attempt to recreate a spirituality that is ancient. So even though its beliefs and practices are pretty new, it is felt that the spiritual core of the religion echoes that of the ways of our ancient ancestors. But along side this; Wicca also attempts to balance this ancient spiritual essence against the push of the modern world, finding a place where the old ways and the new can come together. In so doing, it recognises that although things may change, there are certain things about nature and humanity that are as true today as they ever were.

Since Gerald Gardner came out with Wicca in the 50's it has caused quite a stir and a lot of other witch traditions have emerged that base their views on Wicca. Some even call themselves Wicca in one form or another. In the modern day though, there are effectively only a few kinds of Wicca that trace themselves back to Gardner. The two main ones are known as Gardnerian Wicca (named after Gerald Gardner) and Alexandrian Wicca (created by Alex Sanders, who was a Gardnerian Wiccan).

The God and Goddess

Wiccans worship two deities, whom are most often simply referred to as The God and The Goddess. They are seen to engage in a yearly dance with each other, which takes them on a sacred journey of life and death that mirrors the changing of the seasons and the path that mankind walks as we are born, age, die and are reborn again.

The God

The God, sometimes called "The Horned God" or "The Lord", is a symbol of male power and virility. The Horned God is a culmination of the masculine in nature that has been portrayed in many images (particularly those of horned deities) since Palaeolithic times. The manly imagery of the Wiccan God is the depiction of the ultimate masculine personality. He is young and playful, then virile and sexual, and finally wizened and reflective. This is the truth of the passage of the male life from youth to manhood and then death. The story of the

God's life is told through the yearly cycle of the Sun, beginning at the Winter Solstice where the God is reborn as the Sun and then continues to grow in power until eventually declining again as he ages and the days start to become shorter once more.

Meanwhile, as his life is measured by the passage of the Sun, the person he becomes is revealed through the natural world. He begins his life as the Child of Light, full of promise for the coming year, for a time hidden in the cradled arms of the Goddess. As he grows he becomes a young child, shown to the world in the first emergence of greenery in the land. As the Spring settles in the God takes on the aspects of the wild, emergent world and he plays with the Goddess in high spirits, which is the first stirrings of their romance. At this point he is the young Oak King, ruler of the forest. As he grows further, he falls in love with the Goddess and they are joined in sacred marriage, and the fertile land reflects their sexual joys. Then, as the midsummer Solstice hangs high in the sky, the power of the Oak King reaches its height and the God is mature in life, but with the changing Sun, he is the Oak King no more and now takes on the mantel of the Holly King. The Holly King is wise and old, and he will eventually sacrifice his life for the good of the land, after which he will take his throne in the underworld, where he shall eventually be the protector of the Goddess when she too finally makes her passage through death.

The Goddess

The Goddess, like the God, is embodied through the movements of nature. In Wicca she is chiefly associated with the moon, whose monthly cycle is seen as a symbol of feminine power and a reflection of the Goddess in here three aspects. Fore the Goddess is a triune Goddess, meaning that she reveals herself to us in three forms all at once. These three personas are called The Maiden, The Mother and The Crone, and they are manifestations of the stages of a woman's life as she moves from childhood to old age. As the God is the Sun, she is the Moon and so they are united in their heavenly dance. With the change of the seasons, she joins the God in her various forms, attending him as his mother when he is born, then as his maiden lover when he is grown and eventually she bids farewell to him in her dark aspect as the seasons grow cold at the end of the year.

In her maiden aspect she is young and wide-eyed. At first a child and then a nubile and fertile adolescent, ready to explore the world, indulging in life and love, expressing her journey through the beauty of the natural world. As the Mother she gives birth to everything in nature and then acts to nurture the world. She gives of herself, sustaining the world and helping it to grow through her careful attentions. When the Goddess becomes the Crone, she is old and wise.

She has many lessons to teach about life and magic, guiding us and helping us to learn in the same way that she has done.

The Goddess is the Earth Mother, who has been known by many names and that today is connected to us through Wicca. As the Earth Mother she is the divine womb, from whom all life emerges in our world and indeed, the cosmos itself. But she is not alone in this task. She exists in balance with her consort, the Horned God, and together their sacred love ensures the fertility of creation and its constant renewal from year to year.

The Sabbats

Over the course of a year, Wiccans celebrate a series of seasonal festivals, known as Sabbaths. There are four Sabbaths in the Wiccan year, along with two solstices and two equinoxes, that are also celebrated by the majority of Wiccans. However, the Sabbaths are the major festivals of the religion.

Samhain

The Wiccan New Year begins from the festival of Samhain (pronounced: sow-in) which takes place on October 31st. The day most often associated with Halloween. This is a time of darkness, when the world is cold and dead. This festival reflects this deathly time, as the God is now in the underworld, where he sits as Lord. However, during this time the barriers between life and death are at their thinnest and so the spirits of the other side may travel freely between their world and ours, with the God holding the doorway open for them. So Wiccans celebrate the return of their dead loved ones and commonly enact a feast in which the spirits of the dead are there dining with them. Meanwhile, the Goddess is also passing through the underworld and so the God stands as her protector in his realm. She will be reborn on the other side of death, but for now she is reunited with her love and will eventually go on the pave the way for his return to the world.

The Winter Solstice (Yule)

On or around December 22nd is the Winter Solstice, the longest night of the year and the shortest day. At this point the Sun reaches the lowest point in its power, yet this is the time that the Goddess has prepared for. As the shortest day it is also the turning towards the light half of the year, as from now on the days will become longer and the sun will grow in power. With this rebirth of the Sun, the God emerges from the Underworld, reborn of the Goddess, who now cradles him safely in her arms.

Imbolc (Candlemass)

This is the second major Sabbath of the Wiccan year, occurring on February 1st. At this point the Goddess has truly asserted herself as the mother of the God and she presents him to the world. The fertility of the Goddess and the youth of the God can be seen in the first stirrings of the natural world, as for the first time we begin to notice the return of the green world, though it is not rich in life yet. As the world prepares to renew itself, the Goddess also prepares to renew herself once more by becoming the youthful Maiden in the coming season. But for now, she oversees the emergence of the young Earth.

Spring Equinox (Eostara)

The Spring Equinox takes place on or around March 21st, marking the start of Spring. Having left the arms of his mother, the God ventures into the fields and woodlands of the rejuvenated world and is ready to take his place as Lord of the forest. Winter is truly over and the world has recreated itself in the image of life. Likewise, the Goddess recreates herself in her Maiden form and she explores the natural world that she has given birth to. She is young and full of wonder. She meets the God in the forests and they playfully begin their romance. With the budding of plants, the land is filled with fertility and these two young Gods are gazing upon each other with love and the first stirrings of sexual attraction.

Beltane

At the end of April comes the third major Sabbath. This time acknowledges the love of the God and Goddess in its glorious totality. They are filled with sexual desire and the entire natural world reflects this. Animals mate, flowers blossom and perhaps in the distant woodland one can hear the clash of dear antlers in their prowess as they seek to earn sexual dominance. This is the sacred marriage of the Goddess and the God. He has truly taken his place as the Oak King, ruler of the living forest, while she is his queen. They are lovers and the whole world is ripe with that love. To celebrate these things, the Wicca engage in much gaiety and in the jumping of the broomstick in order to promote fertility. Some may even take part in the traditional European ritual of the weaving of the maypole, which in its phallic aspect, is very suitable for representing the sexual and marital union of the God to the Goddess. This is a time for great celebrations.

Summer Solstice (Litha)

In mirror to the Winter Solstice, this is the longest day of the year (around June 21st), showing the height of the Gods power as his fiery orb holds its position in the sky. But with the longest day begins the turn of the year towards the darker days, as from now the daylight hours will begin to grow shorter. The Oak King, ruler of the forest, must prepare to surrender his throne when the cold moths set in. He is ageing and he knows that he will have to make a great sacrifice soon, yet he is stoic and prepared to meet his fate with dignity.

Lughnasadh (Lammas)

As Autumn takes hold of the land, it is time to bring in the crops. At this time, the Goddess must sacrifice her lover so that the community can survive. As he is the natural world, he must now be cut down in the fields, so that his power can be harvested and consumed. This is the responsibility of the Corn King. He becomes the vessel of humanity's survival in the cold times ahead. But he will not be gone completely. The presence of the God will remain in the sparse greenery of the woodland, which will be his crown in death as he adopts the mantel of the Holly King, leaving the evergreen plants as a legacy to his power.

Autumn Equinox (Mabon)

At the Autumn Equinox, around September 21st, the Sun's power is balanced between light and dark. This is the time of the second harvest. The Oak King is now completely cut down and stands face to face with what he will become, the Holly King. Their power is equal in the sun, and yet the future is inevitable. So the God slips into death after today and assumes his new position, taking up his crown as the Holly King. The Holly King opens his arms to the coming darkness and allows it to dominate the world, bringing it closer to his kingdom, so that when the wheel of the year returns us to Samhain his world and the mortal world shall touch and he will be reunited with the Goddess once more.

Esbats

As well as the Sabbaths, Equinoxes and Solstices, Wiccans also perform monthly rituals known as Esbats. These rituals normally occur on either the full moon or the new moon and seen as excellent times for spell casting. Where the Sabbaths have a large amount of significance for the God, the Esbats are truly the time of the Goddess, as under her watchful moonlit vigil, she oversees the magics of the coven. The type of magic performed at an Esbat will usually be connected to which moon it is held under, as different moons are seen as being beneficial for different kinds of spell work. But an Esbat also helps bring the coven into further unity by allowing them to meet regularly and share their energies.

Witchcraft

Wicca is the religion of Witchcraft and as such it forms a major part of what Wicca is. Indeed, a person cannot practice Wicca without also practicing witchcraft, as it makes up the very fabric of Wiccan Ritual itself.

Through the ages the term "witchcraft" has meant different things to different people and usually held negative connotations. However, through Wicca, the word "witch" has been reclaimed and essentially transformed, moving it from its ancient connections and bringing it to the head of a philosophy centred on spiritual development and modern ethics. Indeed, the ethics of modern witchcraft can be very broad and personal, reflecting opinions that are as different as people themselves. However, it can certainly be said that witchcraft, whether Wiccan or otherwise, is a practice that these days reflects the needs of modern humanity in its many forms.

Witchcraft covers a large variety of practices, mostly centred around traditional magic and folklore. It can include herbalism, creating charms, making and breaking curses, scrying, dealing with faeries and spirits, prophecy and even medical care. Today, Wiccans speak of "raising power", which is a colourful term that describes how they tend to work their magics. Raising power for the Wiccan witch is a matter of using rituals that seek to align the power of the coven, bring it to its peak and then direct it to a purpose. Though, there is nothing to stop a Wiccan from working their own magic without aid, if they should feel the need.

The magic of Wiccan witchcraft tends to exist in two forms: spells and rituals. Spells are specific magics that are crafted for a prearranged purpose. It could be argued that all magical acts are spells in their own right, though spells tend to have a more disposable quality, being used and then possibly never needed again. Rituals, however, are repeated and always maintain their structure each time they are done. The most obvious magical ritual in Wicca is known as "Circle Casting". This involves creating an area of magical safety in which other rituals and spells can be worked, with the Magic Circle keeping the energy contained within until such a time as the witches decide that they wish to direct it outwards to its purpose.

These rituals make up the heart of Wiccan practice, which is why witchcraft is essential to Wicca and why it is referred to as a "witch-religion", because that is exactly what it is: a religion of witches.

The Wiccan Rede

At the centre of Wiccan practice lies an ethical statement known as the Wiccan Rede. The Rede is a guideline that is intended to offer members of Wicca a principle objective for the way they live and the manner in which they use witchcraft. The Wiccan Rede is just eight words, yet these eight words have inspired a fair number of poems dedicated to it. Sometimes people confuse these poems as being the Rede itself, but in actuality the entire Rede is just this simple verse:

"An it harm none, do as thou will."

Or modernised:

"If it harms none, then do as you will."

It's a simple concept, but it does the job. The meaning of the Rede is that in our endeavours, we should try not to commit harm. If no one is being harmed by what we are doing, then there is no reason you shouldn't do it if you so choose.

However, the Rede is just a guideline, not a law. That is exactly what the word "Rede" means. If you think about it, that makes a lot more sense. It is impossible to not cause harm in life and in some circumstances, causing harm is essential. Wicca is a nature based religion and so it's worthwhile to consider how harm and love both form an equal balance in maintaining the cycles of nature. Animals hunt, kill, fight and all for the greater benefit of their species, while at the same time they also mate, nurture their young and form supportive communities or packs. So the Rede is interpretable and it is left up to the individual to determine what exactly is harmful and what exactly is necessary. So where this helps a person to understand what actions should be taken, it also helps them to understand when no actions should be taken at all. This is especially true in magic. For, although we may seek to use magic to try and make our lives easier, it is worth keeping in mind that sometimes it is the bad things in life that teach us the greatest lessons and that trying to avoid them could be depriving you of something hugely beneficial. This, in turn, can be its own kind of harm. Because when we consider doing "no harm" it is important to include ourselves in that, by making sure that *we* aren't being harmed by our actions either.

Threefold Return

The idea of Threefold Return is also a part Wiccan philosophy. Threefold Return is the idea that anything you do, good or bad, will come back to you threefold. This concept follows along the lines of the familiar mantra of "you reap what you sow", basically telling us that we must be mindful of the results that our actions will bring about.

But what exactly does the idea of "threefold" actually mean?

Well, in some regards it is a literal x3, saying that the actions we take will bring back to us a result that is (figuratively) three times as potent. So in this way there is great reward for positive actions, while negative actions bring to us even worse consequences. A lot of the time this is very true, like how a reputation may spread. Doing good things for people will often earn you a good reputation among even more people and they will be much more inclined to trust and like you in the future, even if they haven't met you yet, while the reverse is true of a bad reputation. When one earns a bad reputation for oneself, it tends to spread quickly and it is taken on board by more people than just the person you may have injured.

But sometimes threefold return isn't always literal. Sometimes it is more figurative. If we keep in mind that Wicca is a religion of balance, we can see how the idea of threefold is merely an expression of that balance. Three is a number of completeness, particularly in Wicca. Three aspects of the Goddess, three incarnations of the God (Oak King, Corn King and Holly King), as well as more general concepts like past, present and future. In this way "threefold" can be seen to be a concept of completeness, saying that the actions we take will come back to us in totality and that there is no way to avoid them in the long run.

When the concept of the Threefold Return is combined with the Wiccan Rede, it helps to keep those in the Wicca ethically grounded, by considering their actions and what the results will be, whether those actions are physical, verbal or magical.

An Overview

All in all, Wicca is a religion of personal responsibility and exploring the divine through nature. It uses witchcraft and ritual to explore the mysteries within initiation and form a close connection with others in the faith.

Useful sources

For further information on Wicca and witchcraft, you may want to check out these useful sources:

Wicca: A Comprehensive Guide to the Old Religion in the Modern World, by Vivianne Crowley

Circle of Fire, by Sorita D'Esté

Witchcraft for Tomorrow, by Doreen Valiente

A Witches Bible: The Complete Witches Handbook, by Janet & Stewart Farrar

Pagan Generation

Druidry: the Spirit of the Land

Among the many Pagan religions, Druidry sits as one of the most popular. Its reverence for the land and mythical genius continues to attract a great many followers. But Druidry isn't all robes and standing stones. It is a spiritual path that takes a combination of hard work, reverence for the land and a sense of style.

What is Druidry?

When asking what Druidry is, it is perhaps important to first establish what Druidry isn't. Firstly, Druidry is not Wicca. It has no real connection to Wicca and doesn't particularly have any great connection to witchcraft either. Secondly, modern Druidry is not a recreation of the practices performed by the ancient Druids. Modern Druidry certainly draws inspiration from that source as a fundamental part of its make-up, but in reality we know so little about the ancient Druids that recreating their ways is nigh on impossible.

Now that we have that out of the way, we can begin to discuss what Druidry really is. Well, Druidry is often described as a religion, and in some cases this is certainly true, but to true and simply pigeon hole it as "another religion" is to do it a disservice, as modern Druidry is much more than that. It is a philosophy, community position, a learned art and above all else, it is a way of life.

Following the spiritual path of the Druid is a way to gain a keener insight into the truth of the world around you, while at the same time serving the land and your community. Indeed, the path puts a great degree of focus upon the responsibilities that come with the Druidic path. It isn't simply about worshipping certain Gods and performing certain rituals, the role of the Druid is to serve the land, to revere it, earn from it and give back to it.

What do Druids do?

A common image of a Druid is that of a robed man, standing in some place like Stonehenge, performing some kind of eldritch ritual. In some regards this isn't too far from the truth. Druids do actually use Stonehenge and other similar place in their modern rituals, in acknowledging certain solar events, such as the Solstices.

But that really is just the smallest piece of the pie.

Druids today perform these priestly functions, but they are also trained to be artists, storytellers, community advisers and teachers. Through their ways, Druids seek to gain an inherent understanding of the truth of our reality, which may be expressed through the natural world, mythology and connecting to the divine.

Druidry is also a green path, in that it holds a very special appreciation ad reverence for nature and the land. In some regards Druids are like custodians of the land in which they live, learning its lessons and keeping it maintained, like an ever-watchful spiritual gardener. This respect for the land often goes well beyond a simple appreciation of the landscape, though. It is also a respect for the spirits and Gods that are local to the land. The Druid understand that concept of community and recognises that they live alongside the spirit world and so those local spirits may be seen as neighbours to be respected as much as you would any human resident.

We are all one in nature.

What do Druids believe?

This is an awkward question to answer, as Druidry isn't a religion in the traditional sense of the word. Although Druids do have a defined outlook and philosophical approach to life, there is no central concept of the divine to which all Druids adhere. So that means that there are no set "Gods of Druidry" and no singular manner in which to approach and worship the divine. Indeed, not all Druids concern themselves with Gods at all. Druids often fit themselves into their local pantheon of Gods and spirits, so a British Druid could worship ancient Celtic deities, while an American Druid may honour the divine in the form of the local Native American concept. Alternatively, each individual Druid may simply align themselves with which ever pantheon of Gods they feel the most comfortable with. It is probably true to say that a reverence of the ancient European (particularly Celtic) Gods is among the most common to Druidry and many Druids concern themselves with these mythologies and forming a relationship with these Gods.

However, it is fair to say that all or most Druids believe in the following things:

1   Life itself has a spiritual nature about it.
2   Nature is sacred.
3   There is more than just the world we see. There also exists a spiritual world around us that we go to when we die, but we may also visit this place for a time in dreams, trances, meditations and other altered states of

consciousness.
4   Rebirth. The Druid concept of reincarnation holds that the soul may be reborn life after life, and that we exist in the spiritual world between lives.
5   The truth of reality is hidden behind our perceptions and can be revealed through study and insight.

Ecology

Druidry is a nature based religion that teaches us to get back in contact with the land and learn of the sacred treasures that lie there. In this way the path teaches that the land itself has valuable lessons to teach us and that it can awaken out spiritual selves by forging a connection to the natural world around us. So all of nature becomes a vessel for exploring our spirituality.

But it is not just a matter being at one with nature, it is also a respect for the heritage and magic of the land that can be found at sacred sites, some made thousands of years ago by our distant ancestors. These sites provide us with a connection to our ancestors and the sense of their spiritual practices, so that we might better understand the wisdom of the land as it was known to them. Though there are other aspects of their ancient ways that are also still detectable in the form of various lore that has been passed down and recorded over time, granting us a connection to our ancestors and the way in which they understood the spiritual side of nature. This is the lore of trees, animals and places, often found in old superstitions and local myths and legends.

All these things provide the Druid with a way in which to form and develop a spiritual connection to the world around them and this, in turn, creates a relationship of respect with that world.

Becoming a Druid

Walking the Druid path isn't actually as simple as it may sound. It actually takes years of study and hard work. In modern Druidry there is a series of advancement and the title of "Druid" is reserve only for those that have advanced to the highest level. There are three such series of advancement, known as Bard, Ovate and Druid.

Bards

A Bard is one who has learned the ways and stories of the Druidic path, as well as possibly local and personal tales. In many ways this is a very difficult thing to do, as a Bard is expected to learn a great myths and legends by heart, so that he can recite them as needed. It is also common for a Bard to have to learn different aspect of lore, such as tree lore and animal lore, and in some cases a Bard would even be expected to learn the lineage of his people (either within his Druidic order or his community).

Ovates

Ovates are masters in herbal lore, which gives them insights into the mystical and medicinal properties of various plants. This is not really witchcraft, however the Ovate does recognise that some plants may be utilised for their magical properties. In this way the Ovate gains a closer understanding of nature an in many ways becomes a healer and apothecary too.

Druid

Becoming a Druid means that you have reached the highest rank on the path and may now be regarded as vastly learned in the ways of the land, community and the Other World. A Druid is considered wise enough to teach others who are on the path and act as an advisor, judge and overseer. Not all Druidic groups adhere to this structure of advancement, but it is the most common in the British Isles, as laid out by the Order of Bards, Ovates and Druids (OBOD). However, practitioners in the U.S. are almost certainly likely to belong to a different group such as Ár nDraíocht Féin (ADF), who uses a different system of advancement whereby a person's studies are more directed in a particular area, as a member of a Guild.

For those seeking to enter into Druidry, they will have a much easier time than with many of the other Pagan religions. Druids are thankfully quite well organised and have large organizations that a person can contact to find out more. Here are a few to get you going:

1   The British Druid Order, PO Box 1217, Devizes, Wiltshire SN10 4XA
    http://www.britishdruidorder.co.uk/home.html

2   The Insular Order of Druids, Membership Secretary, c/o Labyrinth, 2 Victoria Road South, Southsea, Hants PO5 2DF
    http://insular.org.uk/
    http://insular.org.uk/MessageBoard/index.php

3   The Order of Bards Ovates and Druids, PO Box 1333, Lewes, East Sussex BN7 3ZG
    http://druidry.org/

4   Ár nDraíocht Féin

http://www.adf.org/core/

An Overview
Druidry is a modern way of life that connects us to the ancient poetic heart of the land. It brings us back in touch with nature and teaches us to use our natural gifts, so that we can better serve ourselves, our community and the land around us.

Useful sources
For further information on Druidry, you may want to check out these useful sources:

The Druid Way, by Philip Carr-Gomm

The Book of Druidry, by Ross Nichols

The Druids: A History, by Ronald Hutton

The Druids, by Stuart Piggot

Religio Romana: The Spirit of Rome

The ways of the ancient world are not lost to us. Neither are they trapped in frozen stone buildings like the Coliseum, or the carved statues in museums. The classical world is alive with spiritual vitality and the mantel has been taken up by a modern generation of Pagans, who respectfully follow the Gods of one of the greatest Empires that our world has ever known.

The New Heart of the Empire

The Religio Romana (the Roman Religion) is the modern embodiment of the ancient spiritual practices of the Roman people and an exaltation of their way of life. It is a reconstructed religion, which means that it does all it can to follow the religious ideals, practices and philosophies that were actually held by the citizenry of ancient Rome. Followers of the Religio Romana construct their religion using genuine literature and records from the time and through the careful examination of archaeological evidence from the same period. The aim is to be as authentic as possible, while still allowing a certain amount of common sense to fill in any blanks and modernise where appropriate.

Following the path of the Romana is not simply taking Greek deities and celebrations, then adding a Latin touch. The Roman religion was far more than that, having been fundamentally based on ideas and Gods that were important to the Latin peoples long before their absorption of certain Greek theologies. It is certainly difficult to know for sure how the earliest Latins viewed their religion, though we know that they were influenced by the Etruscans, to whom they were neighbours (and one time subjects). However, it is not necessary to properly understand the exact details of early Latin religious beliefs, what is important is to know that they are there and to realise how these beliefs were enhanced by their society, as it is certainly true to say that they held certain cultural ideals that they strove to maintain and that these ideals seem to have been equally important when it came to religion. This is why the Roman mentality (or Roman philosophy) is crucial to recreating their religious values, as the Roman religion is directly intertwined with Roman society.

Perhaps the most notable way to which the Romans approach their religion, was expressed through their very legal and balanced attitudes of personal conduct. The Romans were an extremely legalistic people, with a requirement for things to be done in their appropriate way and without chaotic deviation. They were also a people who believed in the division of classes in society, but at the same time that society existed as a single unit, in which the wealthy and influential were expected to serve the needs of the less fortunate members of society, but at the same time, those lower classes were expected to adhere to a certain level of honourable loyalty to those above who were serving them. A society in balance. This gives a good introduction for how the Romans approached their Gods. To them, there were certain ways in which worship should be done and these were the ways that the Gods expected Rome to do it. So if all the rituals and offerings were performed in accordance with these expected practices, thus serving the Gods with respectful honour, then the Gods would in turn serve those who worship them. Thusly, a balance is created.

Pax Deorum

Relationships with the Gods were in many ways akin to business arrangements. Each God was a sovereign to their own area of speciality, much the same as a cobbler is the best authority on how to make shoes and a baker is the best authority on how to make cakes. In a similar way, the Roman Gods would be beseeched for the certain things within their understood area of authority. The appropriate sacrifice or offering would be made and the God would uphold their end of the bargain proceeding to provide a positive influence in the appropriate area of the individual's life. In this way, a person may find themselves following different deities for different reasons at different times. But similarly, such offerings need not be on such an individual level. Very often those in positions of power may give large offerings to the Gods for the benefit of their greater society, or alternatively many individual may make lesser offerings to (in effect) create a larger collective offering that would benefit the entire city, state or Empire. So it was that all the Gods received worship across the various levels of society and the Gods, in turn, upheld their end by granting their followers the favour of their influence. Thus the Pax Deorum was upheld – the "Peace with the Gods".

A Family Faith

The heart of Roman faith was (and is) always very much centred around the family and the home. Although various Gods may have been looked to at certain times and for certain favours, each family retained a permanent connection to their own God or Gods. Each household would contain a shrine to their family Gods and this would be constantly maintained throughout the year, for both the benefit of the house and the honour of those Gods who served it.

Along with the honouring of the Gods within the home, Roman families would very often pay similar homage to ancestral guardian spirits who were seen to be the protectorates of not only the house, but also of individuals and the family line. Sometimes these may be viewed as ancestral spirits who have been elevated to a place of prominence, or possibly as the "Genius" of the family or home, which is kind of the spiritual embodiment of everything that the family is. It would be very easy to reduce the concept of the Genius to something much like a guardian angel, but although this may be accurate in some regards, it is also seriously undervaluing the role and position of a Genius. The Genii (plural of Genius) cover a large variety of beings:

Genius: The individual Genius may be regarded differently at different points in history. Originally, a Genius was seen as the spirit of a deceased ancestor who took on the responsibility of being the spiritual guardian of their family line. However, in time the concept of the individual Genius developed and became more personal, so that the Genius was more viewed as a personal spiritual guardian, much as we would consider the term "guardian angel". But even this would be a deceptive description, for the personal Genius is not merely an entity separate to the individual, it is also a part of them, perhaps best described as their "Higher Self" or their "Divine Self". In this guise, every man was believed to have a Genius and the female equivalent was called a Juno.

Genii Loci: The Genii Loci are the "spirits" (for lack of a better word) of places and things. The Genius in this regard extended beyond the individual, to be the embodied spirit of a place and was often depicted as a snake. Unlike the individual or family Genius, the Genii Loci do not necessarily possess any kind of protective or guardian qualities and their personalities are more often noticed through the "feel" of a place.

Lares: In some ways the Lares (or Lar, if singular) are a unique kind of blending between the personal Genius and the Genii Loci. They are better discerned as household Gods in many cases, though in others they are better seen as spirit beings of a lesser order (sometimes connected with other locations in a similar way to Genii Loci). When we speak of the household Gods in Roman religion, it is the Lares that are being referred to. However, their placement as "Gods" is a tricky one, as the Lares were viewed differently at different points in history. Originally they were closer to what we may call Gods, but in a manner much like that of the Genii Loci. They were only connected with one small place (like the Genii Loci), but received family worship as one may give to a God. However, later the concept of the Lares became connected to that of Manes, who were the most virtuous dead within a family line. In this, the Lares were sometimes viewed as the virtuous dead who had been elevated to a prominent status as household guardian spirits. In this capacity, they have also been known as "Penates".

Within households, the Lares were represented by a small statue and were assumed to be involved in all things that took place there. These statues were given offerings and thanks, as it was believed that if the family neglected the Lares then they would turn their back on the family and protect it no longer.

Religion in the here and now

Roman religion was very much concerned with immediate and the immanent. These people lived in the real world and had current concerns; thusly their dealings with the Gods were truly rooted in their current lives. The Religio Romana does not deal in concepts of mystical metaphysics; in fact it may be true to say that it is more of a "hands on" religion of life. There is little concern given to concepts like the future of the universe, the destiny of the soul or the meaning of life. Instead the Religio Romano deals in practical application, based on the idea that our lives are connected to the lives of the Gods and that by paying them due service they, in turn, will treat us with equal regard.

But the Roman religion is also a very accessible religion and the Romans themselves were extremely adaptable. Their religion was (and is) a syncretic one, meaning that it had no trouble in existing alongside other beliefs and very often allowed the individual the opportunity to meet their other spiritual needs by adopting the religious philosophies or practices of foreign cultures, such as the Greeks, Celts, Egyptians or other more oriental sources. It is worth noting that this is not eclecticism. Eclecticism would be to borrow from different sources and combine them, thus creating something new and unique. Roman syncretism was to follow the Roman religion, as well as allow for separate religious philosophies and Gods to exist alongside it – not combine with it. Though it is true that the Romans did take elements of other religions into their own and that they often equated foreign Gods with their own, the prior was the result of a slow cultural change, not immediate attempts to alter their religion, while the latter was as much political as it was spiritual. Indeed, their recognition of foreign Gods as being like their own was not an attempt to absorb the religious practices of other cultures into their own, instead it was a way in which they could co-exist and understand foreign cultures, and possibly how their own Gods exist to other peoples.

This begins to outline some of the chief concerns that influenced Roman thought and thus, Roman religion. The Romans were very concerned about community and how their society could be at its best. They generally sought to co-exist with other faiths (so long as those religions maintained the peace) and to promote certain community values that served the welfare of society. To them, that society and the values that should be sought after, began at home and from there radiated out to the rest of society, regardless of class of station.

Roman Virtues

The values that were exalted by the Romans were not about attaining wealth as a status symbol, nor were they about fame and they certainly were not a list of orders from the Gods. Instead the Roman Virtues were ideals to strive for that gave an individual moral strength and dignity of character. They were not about individual salvation, they were about the betterment of society and the upholding of civilisation.

> **Auctoritas:** The earned recognition of an individual's position in society, that brings with it the respect for who they are and what they have achieved.
>
> **Comitas:** A good, approachable nature and being of good humour.
>
> **Clementia:** A merciful and forgiving nature.
>
> **Dignitias:** The ability to recognise the value of oneself and take pride in who you are and what you have achieved.
>
> **Firmitas:** Being the kind of person who knows their own mind and sticks to it with a stalwart nature.
>
> **Fruglitas:** To be well versed with money and expenditure, treading that wise ground between excessive and miserly.
>
> **Gravitas:** To understand the importance of things and approach them with the earnest sense of responsibility that they deserve.
>
> **Honestas:** Portraying oneself as a respectable member of society
>
> **Humanitas:** Being civilised, cultured and willing to learn. A certain refinement of character.
>
> **Industria:** To be hard working.
>
> **Pietas:** To respect your place in society and the place of others, while acknowledging the responsibilities that come with it.
>
> **Prudentia:** The wisdom of discretion and keen judgement.
>
> **Salubritas:** To be clean, healthy and hygienic.

Severitas: The ability to remain calm and collected in the face of problems, so that you may wisely and correctly.

Veritas: To be true to your word when dealing with others.

These personal virtues should be sought to be maintained by each individual, but beyond these personal virtues are certain society virtues which every Roman should seek to embody at a greater level. Many of these societal virtues are simply extensions of the personal ones in some form or another, but in addition to these there also some additional ideals which a society should seek, such as: Freedom, Prosperity for everyone, the acknowledgement and celebration of good times, the maintaining of hope in bad times, Peace between all in a society and harmony with other nations, courage, Justice amongst all levels of society, and of course, the honouring of the Gods.

To the Romans, all these traits were not merely desirable traits of humanity, but defining features of what it meant to be Roman. These days the virtues are equally important to those following the Roman Gods, whether they are of Roman descent or not. This is what made the Romans worthy of the Gods in the past, and they are the aspired virtues under the Gods today. This is perhaps the ultimate example of how Roman religion and Roman society are directly connected: Their relationship with the Gods was a reciprocal arrangement – the Gods helped humanity because humanity honoured them. This arrangement existed across society and depended equally on all of society adhering to it. Thusly that society had to be strong and these virtues held it together and demonstrated that they were worthy of the God's attentions. The virtues defined whether or not a person was a "good Roman" and thusly how they were regarded in their society. But the virtues, as a measure of one's worth, were also the bench mark by which a person's life could be measured, which in turn would reflect how each individual would spend their time in the afterlife.

Beyond this world

The Roman religion sees the afterlife as a final reward or punishment that relates to the life you have lived. However, it also embraces the idea of reincarnation. In this way the Roman afterlife is one of many different levels, best summed up as The Elysian Fields, Asphodel and Tartarus. These different realms and what occurs there are effective punishments or rewards for living a life that is either good or bad, and pleases or displeases the Gods.

The Elysian Fields
This is what can effectively be referred to a "paradise" for the soul. The final resting place for the best of mankind. The Elysian Fields are reserved for the most virtuous of mortals and those that have proven themselves as noble warriors and heroes. Virgil described the Elysian Fields (also called Elysium) as a place of perpetual Spring, where the sun always shines in the day and a man may take rest under the shade of beautiful trees and at night the sky was decorated by its own stars. While Pindar describes Elysium as the dwelling place for those that have lived three blameless lives.

Asphodel
The meadows of Asphodel were reserved for the ordinary souls of mankind, where they could continue to live a good life as a Shade. The Romans drew from the Greeks for much of the afterlife imagery, though often with a few alterations to make them more accommodating to the Romans. Of course, this is perfectly acceptable, as the Gods would surely wish to reward the good Roman in the most appropriate way. The Asphodel Meadows entered the mythology from the Greeks, to whom it was a place filled with Asphodel flowers – the favourite food of the Greek dead.

Tartarus
Those of you familiar with the Bible may already have heard of Tartarus, as the word and concept entered into Christian thought and is commonly interpreted as Hell. The depiction is not too far off, but although Tartarus is a place of punishment, it is not a place of eternal punishment. Souls of the most wicked people and those that have offended the Gods, are sent to Tartarus, where they are punished until they have paid for their offences. It was a place where the walls were unbreachable and it flowed with rivers of fire. In the middle was Tisiphone upon a tower, whipping everyone.

From time to time Dis (Pluto), the God of the Underworld, or his queen would grant a reprieve to certain souls in these areas of the underworld and allow them to drink from the waters of forgetfulness so that they may return to life on Earth. This was especially true of those who had died unjustly, such as those who were murdered or that died at a young age. However, the concept of reincarnation proper, was not really one that was universally taken on board by the Romans, instead it was much more common among the Mystery Religions of Rome that came from the East, or that were otherwise influenced by Eastern thought. So although the Romans did sometimes allow for such things, more often they considered the dead in a much more spiritual sense, as either dwelling in the afterlife, like Asphodel or Elysium, or otherwise reflected upon them in the form of the Lares or Penates.

Though it is worth bearing in mind that from the Roman perspective, giving consideration to what happens in this life is far more important than what occurs I the next. As was mentioned above, the Religio Romana is a religion of "now" and the most important thing is to life for now and to use your life to achieve harmony with the Gods and to build a strong life that will benefit people for generations to come.

An Overview
The Religion Romana is a path that exalt the goal of forming a harmonious and prosperous community, while living a virtuous life that allows a person to achieve a sense of peace and balance with the Gods. By serving the Gods (great and small), they in turn serve us. The Religion Romana is about life and finding harmony between our spiritual obligations and our living obligations.

Useful sources
For those wishing to learn more about the Religion Romana, its Gods and the world it comes from, you may wish to check out these useful sources:

The Temple of Sulis Minerva at Bath, by B. Cunliffe

Paganism in the Roman Empire, by R. MacMullen

An Introduction to Roman Religion, by John Scheid and Janet Lloyd

Dictionary of Roman Religion, by Lesley Adkins and Roy A. Adkins

The Roman Household: A Sourcebook, by Jane F. Gardner and Thomas Wiedemann

Heathenry – True to the Gods

Heathenry is a Neo-Pagan religion that attempts to, as best it can, recreate the faith of the ancient Germanic peoples and to follow their Gods in the modern world. There are common images come to mind when Gods like Thor and Odin are mentioned, but Heathenry is a great deal more than Vikings and long boats.

What is Heathenry?

Heathenry is best described as a form of "Germanic Paganism", covering the religious practices of a variety of ancient peoples, such as the Norse, the Anglo-Saxons, Icelanders and the modern expressions of their faiths in the form of movements like Asatru (one expression of the modern Heathen religion).

The core of Heathenry is having faith in the Gods. In fact, that is exactly what Asatru means and I can't think of any way to better describe this wonderful religion. But in addition to faith in the Gods, it is equally important to be of sufficient character that *they* would have faith in us. In order to truly understand Heathenry, it is necessary to know who their Gods are and where they come from. As mentioned, Heathenry is Germanic Paganism or more specifically it is the faith of the ancient Germanic peoples, which has been revived in the modern world through an in depth study of archaeology, folklore and the Norse sagas and poetry – among other sources. Note, Germanic does not mean just Germans. The Germanic people are defined by the possession of the same language group and they stretch from one side of Northern Europe, all the way to Iceland and even discovered America long before Columbus. But what really unites the Germanic peoples (and indeed, the modern followers of Heathenry) is a shared culture and the Gods of that culture.

The Gods

You may already be familiar with some of the Germanic Gods, if not from hearing of their mythology, then probably from popular culture, such as TV shows and comic books. Some may even argue that the use of their Gods in these kinds of things is a testament to the longevity of the Gods and their continued presence in the lives of mankind, who have just been waiting for the right time to rediscover them. I think it is fair to say that either way, the Germanic Gods strike a certain cord in the minds of humanity and even if we don't follow them, we are still able to take pleasure in their tales, even the modern ones.

In examining who the Gods are, it is important to mention that the Germanic pantheon is rather large and that there is no way of sufficiently covering all of the Gods here. But certain deities in the pantheon do take the spotlight more than others and are often highly regarded across the mythology. The second thing that is worth mentioning is that the Gods are divided (or once were) into two different tribes, called the Æsir and the Vanir. At one time these two tribes of Gods were at war with each other, but after fighting to a stalemate, the Gods chose a path of diplomacy and attained peace and unity by exchanging member's of each other's tribes. But this was more than a war time transfer of captives, it was a willing joining of the tribes in a way that unified the Æsir and the Vanir, through ties of trust and in some cases, marriage.

The Æsir

Odin: The first of these Gods is Odin, who gives his name to Wednesday (as he is also known as Woden – Woden's day - Wednesday). Odin is the All Father, chief amongst the Gods, renowned for his wisdom, above all else. However, Odin is also a master of magic and the written word, as he is the one that brought us the Runes, which he discovered through an act of self-sacrifice, having been pinned to the World Tree, Yggdrasil. In many ways this is a prime example of Odin as the father of all, as he is always willing to submit himself to trials and sacrifice in order to retrieve benefits for humanity and the other Gods. His greatness has earned him the position as chief among the Gods.

Balder: This God is renowned for his light, purity, innocence and beauty. He is the son of Odin and Frigg, and was loved by the Gods and humanity, alike. However the majority of stories about Balder concern his death and later resurrection. Balder's death was orchestrated by the trickster God Loki, who was jealous of Balder. But Balder is not the typical God of resurrection, he still lays dead and will only return to life after the world ends and the Gods die in the event known as Ragnarok.

Frigg: Of Frigg it is said that "she knows all fates, but says nothing". This either makes her extremely wise (which would be appropriate for the wife of Odin) in how events will play out, or that she is a gifted seeress (also appropriate for the wife of Odin, who gave us the Runes). She is commonly connected to motherhood and may be called upon in this area.

Thor: "The Thunderer" as some may call him these days, is a mighty guardian God, who protects the mortal realm from being besieged by giants and other similar beings who would otherwise cause us problems. As such he is, of course, a great warrior. He is married to the beautiful Goddess Sif, with whom he has the daughter Trude (whose name means "strength"). Thor's magical hammer, Mjolnir, remains a powerful symbol of faith for Heathens.

Tyr: Tyr, although known to be a great warrior, is most regarded for his outstanding virtue and honour. Tyr has just one hand, as the other was severed by the great wolf Fenrir, who the Gods sought to chain and bind. But the only way that the beast would allow itself to be bound was if one of the Gods placed their hand in the beast's jaws, as a sign of trust (and jeopardy). Tyr allowed himself to be bitten, as he was the most forthright of the gathered Gods and as a result he lost his hand.

Loki: Debate exists as to whether or not Loki should be placed amongst the Gods, as information on him is vague in that regard. But his position as trickster is well established. Many may view Loki in a negative light, while others see him as an essential force that allows us to inspect our customs and motives, often by way of "shock tactics". Regardless of his alignment, he nonetheless does create an atmosphere in which one often has to reassess their preconceptions or learn to guard themselves against weaknesses that they may not have been aware of.

The Vanir
Freyja: Freyja is regarded as a Goddess of female sexuality and love (specifically the rush of love). In this way she is the fierce aspect of a woman. Early in her mythology she has a husband, who dies soon after, but she then becomes a fair example of the relaxed attitude to sex and sexuality among the Vanir, as she is quite wiling to take on lovers at her discretion. In addition to her great sexual appeal, Freyja is seen to be a mistress of magical arts and is sometimes thought to have been the one who taught Odin the arts of magic.

Freyr: Like his sister, Freyja, Freyr has connections to fertility, but his domains are the sun, the rain and the crops. Thusly he is looked to in order to gain a good harvest. Often he may also be looked to for a fertile marriage, but this is perhaps due to his own fidelity in his marriage, which in some ways sets him apart from many of the Gods.

Njord: Father of Freyja and Freyr, Njord is a God of wealth and prosperity; however his field of influence is specifically the sea. Thus he grants the favours of the ocean, fishing and sea voyages. He is a God of the winds and also of fire. Njord is most regarded for marrying the Jotun maid Skadhi, but their marriage ended in an effective divorce and mutual friendship, showing that he is amicable and mature in the field of relationships.

When discussing the Gods of Heathenry, it is most important to discuss exactly how they are regarded amongst their followers. Unlike in many other religions, the Gods are not simply seen as rulers of humanity; no, the Gods are seen to effectively be members of the tribe. Certainly, they are highly regarded and offered praise, but that is an acknowledgement of who they are and what they do for their people. For the Gods are part of the every day lives of a Heathen, just as they were for their ancestors. It is seen that the Gods have existed among their people for many ages and take a direct hand in the lives of the people and gift them with the benefit of their wisdom, history and example. The Gods are part of the community and as such they are treated as honoured friends, allies and family.

Sacred Spirit, Heathen Heart

The Heathen way is not just a path of honouring the Gods, it is also a path that seeks to honour one's ancestors and the ways that they followed. To the Heathen, one's ancestors are to be respected and praised for their great deeds. They are not only the founders of an inherited spiritual tradition, they are also the roots of each of us. Each generation is connected to their ancestors and the destinies that their actions have created for all their descendants. We are who we are because our ancestors set their family down a path that has led to where each of us is today. Into that line of descent they sought to instil certain values and ideas that would make their people strong and maintain their cultural identity.

But veneration of the ancestors is about more than simply acknowledging their achievements. It is about recognising them as a genuine spiritual presence that exists in our day to day lives, much as the Gods themselves do. Our ancestors can be guides or guardians to us, their children, and seeking a close spiritual relationship with them is part of the Heathen way. It is also worth mentioning that to some Asatruar, the Gods themselves are seen as ancestors, viewed as the progenitors of their people and so this becomes an extension of the view of the Gods being family and friends. This approach to the spiritual side of life is very much the underpinning of the faith and living within it. It is the idea that we exist in a spiritual community, where we all have our roles and deserve respect for our accomplishments. Like a community there is a certain element of give and take, but ultimately we should seek to co-exist with out neighbours and raise each other up for our own greatness.

Heathen Virtues

Heathenry – and specifically Asatru - stands tall as not only a religion, but a way of life that seeks to exemplify certain principles that were held sacred to the Germanic people of the past. These virtues are a mark of respect to our ancestors, the Gods and (perhaps most importantly) to each other and ourselves. By following this creed the community is maintained, both physically and spiritually, and you live as a testament to your own honour and worth. These ideals have been embodied in the Nine Noble Virtues of Asatru:

> **Courage:** The acknowledgement that death is inevitable, so it is important to live bravely and meet the challenges of life head on. To live bold in the face of adversity.
> **Discipline:** Showing yourself to be level headed and in command of your own mind, so that you do not let your anger rule you. Instead, you rule yourself and this, in turn, show that you are worthy to lead others.

Honour: To act in a righteous way, even if others do not. This is proving your worth through your own inner integrity, not just because society expects you to.
Hospitality: To accept the privilege of helping your fellow man, by extending what you can afford into the community for those who need it.
Independence: Being self-sufficient, standing on our own feet financially, mentally and spiritually. The ability to think for oneself and take responsibility for your actions.
Industriousness: The willingness to do the work that is needed and strive forwards.
Troth: Living up to your obligations and oaths, thus earning a reputation as someone that can be trusted to keep their word.
Truth: To be honest with ourselves and those around us, or otherwise remain silent as not to mislead.
Steadfastness: To continue, no matter what. The virtue of perseverance and a willingness to go the distance and see things through until the end.

These virtues are self supporting, creating a person who stands firmly because they possess great integrity and strength of character. They are a yardstick through which we govern ourselves and each other, as it is not the Ásatrú way to seek morality from outside. Instead the Ásatrú prove themselves worthy of being part of a community founded by the Gods and of being recognised by their ancestors, not because the Gods demand it, not because their ancestors demand it, but because each Ásatrú should demand it of themselves.

Home and Hearth

One could say that the foundation stone of Heathenry is in the home. It is our families, friends and the way we come together. Plus, some Heathens belong to groups, sometimes referred to as "Hearths" or "Kindreds", who meet for shared rituals and fellowship. To the Heathen, the uniting force at the heart of Heathenry – whether that be the Heathen home or the extended family of friends and Kindred – is Fridh. Fridh (pronounced "frith") is a concept of social unity and responsibility that, when entered into, results in peace and well-being for all in the group. It is a very complex concept in a philosophical sense, and yet ideally simple in it's application. Fridh seeks to unsure the continued peace and prosperity of the social group through the adherence of ideals of social conduct and openness. In the home, each member of the family is expected to fulfill their responsibilities towards the household and towards each other. This then extends into the greater community. At the heart of this is a spirit of reciprocity, i.e. that each member gives to the community and so the community gives to each member.

One key aspect of adhering to Fridh is that of hospitality. Ideally, the Heathen should seek to be a good host to friends, family and those in need. Likewise, the other party should do all they can to be a good guest. Through the maintenance of these social etiquettes, peace in the community is achieved. However, that is also where the concept of Fridh can become complicated, as to an outsider the peace of the community may sometimes appear to be disagreement, dissension and general arguing. For you see, Fridh also encourages the free exchange of ideas and encourages a person to raise their voice on matters. Heathens, like all people, can have a great variety of views on different topics and so it may appear that the community is divided. But in reality, this honest airing of opinions, views and grievances strengthens the community by allowing everyone a voice, encouraging honesty and stopping people from holding private grudges and angers that may grow into something that later threatens social peace and unity. In this way, Fridh encourages the coming together of the community in open, honest and respectful debate, so that the community itself is made stronger. So one can say that Fridh is an active force of community involvement, which each person adds to and as a result, peace in the community is achieved and the bonds between it's members are strengthened.

The Blót

If the community is the centre of Heathen living, then the Blót is the centre of Heathen practice. The Blót is a social gathering that serves as a ritual in which the Gods and ancestors receive raise and offerings. These functions an have various structures, with some being more formal than others, though they all tend to contain the following elements: The Call to the Gods, make offerings to the Gods, Bless the attendees, share the drink. In the first part, the Gods are invited into the gathering in some way. This could be in the form of a prayer or maybe just a spoken declaration to the deities you wish to call. Following this, those in attendance give forth any offering that they may have for the Gods. Very often this will be poured libations of mead, though in some cases offerings may take the form of ritual dramas or some kind of act. Some Heathens may simply bless the mead in the name of the Gods and save the libations for after the attendees are also blessed. Either way, once the offerings are made to the Gods, those gathered may receive a blessing. This is done by sprinkling or dabbing some of the drink onto the gathering, often by using a sprig of greenery. After this, the drink may be passed around the gathering in the traditional drinking horn and each attendant drinks a toast to the Gods. That generally completes the more ritualised aspect of the Blót and tends to be followed by a time of feasting in which the drinking and merriment will continue. Very often, this will lead to a Sumble.

Sumble

The Sumble is a kind of ritualised drinking session that often takes place at Blóts, though can also be a ritual separate and of itself. In a Sumble, the gathered kindred pass the drinking horn amongst them and with each drink it is customary to toast and honour the ancestors, as well as those who deserve similar recognition. In addition to this, the toast is used as a means to bring into being the oaths and intentions that we intend upon fulfilling. This is a very sacred time, the Gods are watching and the words spoken are a contract between the speaker and the listener, in which one boasts of his oaths and the others agree to bear witness to these things. In many ways this is a test of honour and wisdom. The honour of the one swearing the oath is being tested, as they are expected to fulfil their oaths, while the wisdom of everyone there is being tested, as the oath maker should be wise enough to not make oaths he cannot keep and those in attendance should have the wisdom to recognise such oaths and the honour to stop them being made.

Wights and the Land

In the past the Germanic people had very close ties to the world around them. The land in which they lived was ancestral land. The success of crops and hunting depended upon the land providing a good bounty. Similarly, the movements of the weather outlined when crops should be harvested, when it was a good time to sail and may even have served as omens. This is where the beliefs of the Heathens reveal their more animistic connections, as to them, the land was alive with a wealthy of spirits and these spirits, called Wights, could either be a blessing or a curse. The Wights were in many ways also part of the community, as they belonged to the greater community of the land and so it was necessary to seek their blessing when attempting to use that land, for crops, etc. Offerings would be made to the Wights in order to keep them friendly to the people and even today these practices are still maintained as a cultural tradition in places such as Sweden and Norway, where offerings of porridge are given on Christmas Eve.

Not all Wights were seen as benevolent, though. Some were taken to be openly malicious or even dangerous, such as trolls and some giants (though whether giants should be classed as Wights is debatable). In these instances, the people would seek to protect themselves from these negative Wights.

Today, belief in Wights continues in Heathenry, though the need to seek their help in raising crops is perhaps a little less of a concern in the lives of the average person. But Wights are seen to inhabit everything to some degree. Houses, groves, forests, fields, even cities, can all be said to have their resident Wights that may look favourably upon those who seek them out and wish to involve them in their lives. Perhaps the modern mind might even see "gremlins" as malicious techno-Wights of today.

Magic and the Runes

Another aspect of Germanic culture that you may already be familiar with is the Runes. The Runes serve many purposes, including writing, divination and magic. It must be noted, though that although the Runes have magical and divinatory associations, not all Heathens practice these arts. Instead it is better to see these things as another extension of community position, in which all have their skills which they may use for the benefit of their fellows, such as woodwork, metalwork, leadership, farming and in the modern day, computer programming, publishing and any other ability that allows a person to serve well the Heathen community that they associate with. In the case of some people, their skills lay in the areas of Runecraft and magic.

This is not as easy as it may sound. Even the task of reclaiming the magical traditions of the north is a difficult one and like all else within Heathenry, it relies to a great degree on studying the Germanic lore, history, myth and legend. But for those who have put in the work, they are able to make use of a magical system (albeit in a modern way) that effectively dates back thousands of years.

Each and every Rune has multiple meanings, as well as serving as an alphabet. The Runes themselves are not merely a system of divination and magic, but a collected representation of heathen culture in its many aspects, a connection to the Gods, and also the connection between past, present and future. On top of this, the Runes are similar to Tarot Cards, in that their meaning can change from one situation to the next and tend to rely upon context.

Seidh

More difficult to reclaim than the Runes, are the northern magical practices known as Seidh. In some ways, Seidh magic may be compared to the old view of "witchcraft" and "cunning crafts". But unlike witchcraft, Seidh magic was not simply a human discipline. Some Gods were also said to know the ways of Seidh, such as Odin who could use Seidh magic for prophecy, controlling the weather, transformation into animals, inflicting illness, causing death and granting power. For humans, the use of Seidh magic seems to focus on things that are useful to the individual and community, such as bringing fertility to crops or people (as well as removing such fertility), blessing a hunt, and the granting of good or bad luck. The Sagas do speak of the human ability to transform into an animal using such magic, though these days people tend to regard this a spiritual transformation that is accompanied by an out of body experience in the new animal form. This view of it as a spiritual journey seems to be well enforced, as the sagas often depict the traveller having more direct interaction with the Wights while in their animal form, implying that they are on the spiritual level of our reality, rather than the physical.

Seidh magic is generally practiced by entering a trance state in a manner similar to how Siberian Shamans might, as well as their equivalents in other cultures. The common way in which this state is entered is by retiring to a secluded place, wrapping oneself in a cloak and remaining there for several hours so that you may enter the trance state in peace and seclusion. This method appears to be a kind of deep meditation, but through this meditative trance, a person may seek to journey spiritually or commune with the Gods, ancestors and Wights. Contacting one's ancestors in this way could be helped by finding a place close to their spirit, such as a grave, tomb or shrine.

Heathen magic can also be an active, dramatic thing. Whereas seeking to voyage in spirit and commune with the dead appear to have been achieved through slow, quiet means, other magical goals such as weather manipulation could be performed through ecstatic dance and singing. Other magical methods include the use of herbs, the tying of cord and the bringing of nightmares.

A further extension to Seidh magic is a particular kind of prophetic magic that is sometimes called **Spae**. Although the Runes are commonly thought of as a tool for divination, Spae magic is its own unique form of divination and prophecy. This form of prophetic magic has several methods of use, but all seem to rely upon the idea that the individual possesses some kind of innate power or ability to reveal the future in some form. That is to say, they are the means through which the magic works, rather than through the use of the Runes and similar tools. Spae can be used by those that are just naturally "seers" and able to tap their abilities at will. This may be performed by certain supernatural beings or by enigmatic prophets who travel constantly, but serve audiences in a similar manner to the Oracle at Delphi. For those with a less defined natural gift, it may be required that they enter some kind of ecstatic trance in order to "tap into" their prophetic abilities. Others work through a medium, such as reading omens and signs in the world around them.

The Halls of the Gods

Heathen mythology teaches that the living are rewarded for their deeds after they die. All the dead go to the underworld of Hel, ruled by the Goddess of the same name. This is the resting place of most of the Heathen ancestors and is said to be a fairly pleasant place. However, those that have achieved great deeds or proven themselves as somehow exceptional, may become the chosen of the Gods and accepted into their halls in the afterlife.

The most well known to most people is Odin's Hall, call Valhalla. This is the destination for the greatest of warriors and heroes, where they battle all day and feast all night. Though this is not the only option open to the selected few. It has been said that the dead may also go to Freyja's hall if she chooses them and that it is a common destination for women, while unmarried women may go to Gefjun's hall, where she has set aside a chosen place for the chaste. Each God has their hall, or otherwise shares one with their spouse, but not all have a specific myth about those that they are more favourable towards in order to gain entrance to their hall. However, it has been suggested that the Gods may choose their closest followers to sit with them in their halls after death. In this way, the dead spend their afterlife with the God that they connected to most and the sense of family is continued.

But in Germanic myth, the halls of the Gods were not a restriction for the dead, as they have a level of freedom to continue interacting with the living. The dead could attend their own graves and speak to the living in dreams. It is also fair to say that the ancestors may attend other places, as well, when they are being called upon or honoured. In addition to this, among some Heathens is the idea of reincarnation, in which the dead may get to taste life once more by being born again into their own family line. Perhaps this is how the faith of the Gods is being revived, as the old followers are being reborn into their family lines, which have now spread across many countries.

An Overview
Heathenry is a religion of personal conviction in which one serves their community through their personal strength and integrity. With this integrity they come before their Gods and ancestors, to give them honour. The great focus is on one's personal honour, which is the corner stone of every Heathen's worth in their local community and family, as well as the greater community of their Heathen kindred, their ancestors and the Gods.

Useful sources

For further information on Ásatrú, you may want to check out these useful sources:

Northern Magic: Mysteries of the Norse, Germans and English, by Edred Thorsson

Hammer of the Gods: Anglo-Saxon Paganism in Modern Times, by Swain Wodening

Essential Ásatrú, by Diana L. Paxson

Elves, Wights, and Trolls, by Kveldulf Gundarsson

The Runes: The Only Introduction You'll Ever Need, by Freya Aswynn

Leaves of Yggdrasil, by Freya Aswynn

Pagan Generation

Celticism – Recovering the Old Ways

In the modern Pagan Age, there are many paths that have emerged from the inspiration of the Celts, but where this sense of archaic wonder has lead many to new ways, others have gained a spiritual need to reclaim the true path of our ancestors.

Reconstruction

The religious movement most commonly known as "Celtic Reconstruction" is among the youngest of the Neo-Pagan religious movements. It began properly in the early to mid eighties as a response to the popularity of Celtic imagery in other Pagan paths. The rise of Druid religions (such as those discussed earlier) and the inclusion of certain Celtic elements in other popular religions like Wicca, gave rise to a desire in many, to reclaim a spiritual tradition that was more accurate to that of the ancient Celts. Where the modern Druid religions have created their path based on Celtic inspiration and a selection of other sources, Celtic Reconstruction seeks to accurately recreate the ways of the pre-Christian Celts for the modern world.

This reconstructive path is among the more difficult of these kinds of religious paths, as sources regarding ancient Celtic spirituality are actually very few. The only historic writings regarding the Celts come from their Roman invaders and Christian monks recorded certain myths of the Celts, though these were often altered to agree more with Christian ideas. Being as written sources are so few, other areas must be looked to in order to gain a greater understanding of the lives and faith of the Celts. As such, the Celtic reconstruction is also drawn from archaeology, surviving folk customs, poems, songs, post-Christian historical documentation and linguistic examinations. The result of this is a modern creation that attempts to be as close to ancient Celtic practices as possible. This makes Celtic Reconstruction a path of keen inspection, where one must often become a historical detective to build a spiritual path that would well reflect the ways of the past.

Finding the Celtic Spirit

The path of Celtic Reconstruction is not simply an attempt to reclaim the religious practices of the ancient Celts; it is an attempt to reclaim the spirit of Celtic life for the modern world. This means to honour their Gods in the same ways as the ancestors and to also approach life with an attitude that rests upon the ethical and spiritual foundations that were important to the Celts of old. However, the Celts were not a united people. In fact, the Celtic nations spanned a very large area that stretched across Europe, the British Isles and into Ireland. Over the Celtic lands there were many different tribes and communities, all with their own distinct customs and personalities. What unites them all as being "Celtic" though, is a shared language family and a shared culture. It may sound odd to say that they all shared a culture and yet were all different, but the differences tend to arise in things like names and local customs, rather than significantly different world views. For example, the Celts all followed the same central festivals, even though some communities may have celebrated some extra ones. Likewise, many of the larger Celtic communities tended to follow the same Gods (more or less), though did so under different names, with their mythologies differing slightly to be more relevant to each tribe or community. But in addition to this, there were also some Gods that were unique to certain parts of the Celtic lands and find little, if any, expression elsewhere. Because of these regional differences, many followers of the Celtic path try to isolate the practices within a certain area and be as true to those as they can. Sometimes this can be difficult, as knowledge of those ways is often fragmented and so they may have to look further a field in the Celtic community in order to determine appropriate ways to fill in the gaps that are still true to the Celtic path.

A big part of reclaiming the Celtic spirituality is to recreate or adopt the traditions and practices of the Celts. This serves several purposes. Firstly these practices, which are often adopted from folk traditions, stand to be a way of expressing faith. Secondly, they are a way of bringing a certain amount of practical unity to an emerging path that effectively has a great deal of variation in its beliefs. The result is often the construction of customs that can be shared by many Celtic Reconstructionists, even if they have differing opinions about the spiritual meaning behind these things.

Sometimes reconstructionist paths, such as this one, also find themselves turning to "personal Gnosis" in order to gain a greater understanding of the ways of the past and the Gods that are connected to them. "Personal Gnosis" is a short way of describing a spiritual experience that provides valuable insights to the path. This form of revelation tends to exist in three varieties Unsubstantiated Personal Gnosis (UPG), which is a personal revelation about the path, Shared Personal Gnosis (SPG), which is a revelation or insight that has manifest across the community, Confirmed Gnosis (CG), which is when any of the first two later become confirmed through evidence found in historical sources. You may wonder how this kind of spiritual *guess work* (for lack of a better term) can really have any place in a path that is supposed to be based on the real practices of the ancestors. However, it must be noted that there are generally two important factors that are taken into account when evaluating experiences of Personal Gnosis. The first is that the information gained shouldn't contradict known facts about the path. This means that personal experiences are never likely to replace the core of historical research and folklore. The second point of evaluation is that Personal Gnosis should not overshadow established practices. That is to say that if someone has a moving personal experience and wishes to include it in their personal practices, then no one can stop them, however that in no way connects it to the practices of others, who will no doubt require a great deal more convincing before they accept unsubstantiated claims.

Warriors and Poets

There is an informal division of the Celtic path that has been seen to arise: that of a "Warrior Path" and that of a "Poets Path". These are by no means official designations. They are simply an observation that amongst some individuals there is a distinct pull towards warrior deities, and these individuals are commonly well suited to serving their community in an active and assertive fashion, while many others seem drawn to Gods of crafts and song, and in these individuals there is a quality of creativity that can be well used in the community in some form.

Those with an interest in arts, crafts, and other creative and cerebral activities, may follow a Druid path that allows them to hone these skills. Alternatively they may simply set up shop as jewellery makers, weapons forgers, leather workers, metal smiths, or possibly as writers and musicians. For those following a warrior path, there may be an inclination to study martial arts, weapon use or maybe just practical survivalist and hunting skills. Those who have already studied martial arts will no doubt understand the very real spiritual connection that can arise from such things. So it is with those who wish to study the warrior arts on their Celtic Path.
There may be those who do not wish to connect oriental martial arts with their Celticism, finding the two to be intrinsically alien to each other. As such a person may wish to study the fighting styles that have descended down through existing Celtic communities, such as certain types of boxing and wrestling. Alternatively they may seek employment in the police force or armed services. For those wishing to really recapture the warrior ways of the Celts, one may examine the myths of the Celts and histories of their enemies, for clues to how the Celts approached combat and the manner in which they fought. For example, the "Salmon Leap" ability which was recorded of the mythic hero, Cú Chulainn. When compared with historical accounts, this appears to have possibly been a trained method of vaulting over an opponent's defenses, such as a mighty jump that allows the Celt to clear the height of a shield. It may even be possible to blend the two paths, as the Druids were recorded to have been able to make magics for the purposes of battle.

The Other Worlds

Celticism sees the existence of not only our world, but also of the spiritual level of the universe and the realm in which the Gods dwell. But the lines between these different levels of reality are not always so clear and one may at times pass from one to the other, or beings from the other planes may make themselves know in our world. For the Celts, ours is a world of man, spirits and Gods.

Ancestors and Animism

In addition to the Faerie realm and its inhabitants, Celtic spirituality holds a great deal of respect for the spirits of the Celtic ancestors who have gone before. They are not venerated in any kind of divine way, but they are held in high spiritual and personal esteem. But a person need not have Celtic ancestry in order to follow the path of Celtic Reconstruction. Indeed, as the Celtic path is a modern one, it is more accepted that through evolution we are all one blood, even if time may have separated us by skin-tone and geography. All our ancestors are sacred, no matter where we may come from and adopting the Celtic spirituality allows us to show our respect for them and how they have brought us to where we are now.

Additionally, the Celtic path is one that is strongly connected to the land – both where you are now and the lands of our ancestors. This connection is a reflection of how vital the land is, but also it is part of a greater animistic belief. This means that the land itself is seen as something spiritual and is inhabited by many different spirits. To the Celts, the world was possessed of its own vital souls. The spirits of animals, trees, places, streams, etc. all had their own sacred essence. To some modern Celtics, this belief even extends to constructed items. These spirits were (and are) a part of every day life and had personalities all their own. They could be good and helpful or spiteful and annoying, sometimes needing to be appeased or otherwise dealt with in order to maintain a peaceful coexistence with the spiritual landscape of the world.

The Sidhe

A significant part of the Celtic movement is faith in the Aos Si – or "Sidhe" – which may be thought of by most people as "fairies". But this aspect of the faith is not a matter of fairy tales as many people would imagine them, it is about representing "The Good Folk" as they originally were, along with their connections to the Celtic Gods. The word Sidhe (pronounced "shee") has become a familiar term for these beings, but in the Celtic tongue it is more properly said as *Aos Si, Áes Sidhe*, or *Daoine Sith*, which mean "The people of the mounds" and "The people of peace". There are many beings in Celtic Tradition that may be describe as Sidhe, and where one draws the line in distinction is often up to the individual. Sometimes the term is used describe a variety of nature spirits which inhabit the land and should be respected, while more often it is used to describe a specific race of beings who live "under the hills". There are those who believe that this means the spirits of ancestors who have been buried in or around barrows and some believe that the spirits of their ancestors descend into the hills to live amongst the true Sidhe, who are their own race, descended from the Gods. Very often, mythology has been interpreted to mean that the Gods themselves descended below the hills at the end of their time and later became known as fairies, as did all the children that they bore in that underground world of *faerie*.

Regardless of how one may interpret the identity of "The Good Folk", they remain a part of the spiritual landscape that is part of the Celtic worldview and much like land spirits, they may be worked with and given offerings in order to forge good relationships with them and earn their favour. Faerie Lore is considerably extensive, though, spanning from before Christianity to after it and from one side of Europe to the other. It is up to the individual to decide which lore is the most reliable in coming to understand the Sidhe, but through examination of these myths it becomes possible to pick out certain central themes to keep in mind about dealing with the Good Folk. Among these is that when angered, they can be extremely spiteful and dangerous, however, when they are happy they can be very helpful to those people who are good to them. It is also a common theme that they have a severe aversion to cold iron, which they seriously dislike. So it is best to keep such things tucked away when trying to deal with the fae. It is also true that many myths show that the Sidhe are willing to interact with humanity on a very personal level, sometimes even marrying into their families. But it also becomes very clear that there are certain matters of etiquette that must be upheld when attempting to engage in a relationship with the fae. Very often these provisos will be laid done by the individual Sidhe, while others are more universal issues of respect and friendliness.

The Gods

Discussing Celtic Gods is not as simple as one may think. Generally there are certain Gods and Goddess that, in one form or another, span across most of the Celtic lands. At the same time, there may also be many local and tribal Gods that are only worshipped within a small region. The majority of Celtic Reconstructionists tend to focus on following just a few of the Celtic Gods, while still keeping a respectful acknowledgement of others. This tends to manifest as a following of about two of the more widespread Gods, while possibly also following one or two of the Gods who are local to a single area from which they draw much of their practices. For example, one person may draw more from Gaulish culture in creating their path, so they would most likely focus on Gaulish deities in their worship, while another Celtic Reconstructionist may prefer a more Irish approach and so focuses their worship towards the same deities that the Irish

Celts would have. There are literally hundreds of Celtic deities. The only way to find out which of the Gods you are most connected to, is to roll up your sleeves and research them. However, as a place to start, you may want to look at some of the Celtic Gods that are discussed in chapter two of this book.

Druids

When discussing the Celts, many people are drawn to explore the mysterious world of the Druids. However, the path of Celtic Reconstruction has little or nothing to do with any of the modern Druid religions (some of which were discussed earlier in this book). In fact, there are very few people on the Celtic path that would consider themselves to be Druids and even those who do may not be recognised as such by their peers. The reason for this is that as Celtic Reconstructionists attempt to recreate the Celtic ways as accurately as possible, they must acknowledge that so little is known about the Druids of old, that becoming one in that way is nigh on impossible. But we do know enough about them, based on old writings and accounts, to know that the position of Druid was one of high regard and significant achievement.

Druids were not simply priests and there is a good possibility that a person may have been a Druid and yet have had no greater religious responsibility than any other Celt. There was no separate "Druid religion". In fact, the religion of each Druid would have been the same as every other member of his or her community (yes, it is possible that there may have been female Druids). To be a Druid was to simply be a member of a certain class of the society, just as we may use the word "aristocracy" to describe a certain class of people. The class of the Druids was made up of the true intellectuals of society who had gained their high status by being recognised for their knowledge, intellect and wisdom. Rather than being just priests, the Druids could be Priests, Law makers, Healers, Historians, Ministers, Scholars, Poets, Magicians, Teachers, etc. The likelihood is that a Druid would have actually been a specialist in more than one area of knowledge, much like how some people these days may have several Degrees in different fields, while also having a Doctorate in another. Caesar records how the Druids were consulted by the leaders of Celtic tribes and so there is a good certainty that the Druids had a good deal of political status and power within a tribe. One may actually call them politicians (amongst other things).

The picture that we have formed of the Druids comes from a combination of Greco-Roman sources (that are quite questionable) and from references in myths and stories. This gives us an idea of the kind of function that they probably served in Celtic society, but we know very little about exactly how they fulfilled that role. If the Romans are to be believed without question, then it would appear that the Druids were the leaders of ceremonies and advised the chieftains of the tribes. However, these same sources also tell of the Druids committing acts of human sacrifice, which could simply be Roman propaganda, much as they did against all their enemies during war time. It is certainly true to say that as of this time, there is little archaeological evidence to suggest that the Druids were engaged in any kind of widespread human sacrifice and the evidence that does exist could easily be interpreted in many other ways. For this reason, Celtic myths and legends are good place to turn to. Despite the fact that these are mythical stories and often come to us second hand, the originals do come directly from the Celts themselves and so they can allow us to glean the realities of the Druids as the Celts would have seen them. This method is also far from perfect, but a lack of other sources produces a need to be creative with what we do have.

However, it is worth noting that although the subject of the Druids and their ways may be debatable, it matters little to the Celtic spiritual path, as the aim is not to produce another neo-Druid religion. The aim is simply to learn as much as possible about the ancient Celts, so that their spiritual way of life may be recreated in a modern context.

Holidays

Traditionally the ancient Celts celebrated four great fire festivals in a year, which generally centred around the lighting of torches and/or a large central bonfire. These events are most commonly known as Samhain, Imbolc, Bealtaine and Lughnasadh, and you may already be familiar with these names, as they have been adopted into other Pagan paths, such as Wicca. However, although religions like Wicca may have adopted these festivals by name and date, they have not adopted them in a Celtic style of practice. Further, although these names are the most common, they are not the only way in which they are known in the Celtic tongues and so some Celtic Reconstructionists may prefer to call these festivals by the same names that would have been used in particular Celtic regions.

Samhain – October 31st
(Calan Gaef, Trinouxtion Samonii, Kala-Goanv, Oie Houney)

By common identification, Samhain marks the beginning and end of the Celtic year, though more accurately it can be seen as the traditional end of the dark half of the year and the beginning of the light half at the start of a new cycle. This festival is a time of endings, beginnings and the void between. The crops are completed and animals are brought in from pasture, seeing the end of farming for that year and the preparation to survive the colder months ahead. Between this ending and the start of the new year, there was seen to be a time of suspension in which the dead may return and time itself looses its usual dominion, becoming more mutable and accessible. As such the dead were welcomed into the homes of the families so that that could share in a feast, while at the same time evil spirits were kept away. During these festivities it would have been common to engage in fortune telling and to also give offerings of animal blood to the land spirits, so that they may help the fertility of the land in the new farming year.

Imbolc – Febuary 2nd
(Oimealg, Lá Fháile Bríde, Goel Kantolyon, Oimelc)

The name "Imbolc" derives from a Celtic root meaning "ewe's milk" and the festival itself has similar connections to milking. Originally Imbolc was set to coincide with the lactation of ewes, which was one among many signs of fertility in the lad at this time, heralding the commencement of life and the mid-point in the light half of the year. This feast is commonly known as The Feast of Bridget and indeed, she is the Goddess to whom this day is most connected. She is connected with the well-being of the tribe, but also is a Goddess of the land and so she is truly the most appropriate of the Celtic deities to preside over this time of year, which focuses on the returning fertility of the land and the tribes return to farming.

Bealtaine – May 1st
(Bealtainn, Boaldyn, Calan Mai, Calan Me, Kala-Mae)

In many ways, the celebration of Bealtaine mirrors that of Samhain, which sits opposite it at the other side of the yearly cycle. Both make use of a ritual bonfire, both utilise the imagery of a wild hunt and both involve a degree of interaction with the supernatural worlds. However, in the case of Bealtaine the contact with the Other Worlds is in the form of interacting with the world of Faerie. This time of year mars the grand victory of light, but also the end of its reign as soon after will begin the darkening of the year. But the high point of this celebration is the lighting of the purifying fire and the sacred marriage between the God Maponos and his Flower Maiden, who is a represented by the relevant Goddess of the Land from the local Celtic mythology.

Lughnasadh – August 1st
(Lúnasa, Lúnasdal, Calan Awst, Laa Luanys)

The final festival of the Celtic year sees the culmination of all previous themes, as the tribe also receive the rewards of their efforts through the year, by reaping the harvest. The name of this festival is taken from the God Lugh, marking the instigation of funeral games introduced by the God in order to commemorate the death of his foster mother, Tailtiu. Lugh is the God of the Tribe and this time of the year represents the success of the tribe in its relationship with the land. Here the tribe itself is celebrated and Lugh, as God of the tribe, is honoured with dramatic enactments and fertility rites. As the victory of the tribe is celebrated it comes together in Assembly, which gives a opportunity for trade and the display of handicrafts. But more importantly, it serves to unite the tribe and strength the bonds between its people.

These are the four central Celtic holidays, however some Celts also celebrated the Solstices and Equinoxes. This only appeared to occur in some Celtic communities, so some on the Celtic Path also choose to follow them, especially if they base their practices on those communities. But modern Celtic practise are not restricted to these eight holidays. Indeed, there is nothing to stop you from enacting your own rituals and rites at a time that holds personal meaning to you, perhaps observing the cycle of nature where you live or to mark an important event in your own life.

An Overview

The path of Celtic Reconstruction allows us to feel connected to the old ways and the old Gods of the Celtic people. It is a way to honour our ancestors and feel closer to who they are and in so doing, better understand who we are and how we can relate to the powers of nature and the divine. Celtic spirituality invites us to find the poet in our hearts and the warrior in our soul, so that we may know our place in the world and live our lives to the fullest. The modern Celt becomes a knowledgeable sage, learning the old ways and in doing becomes the master of his own ceremonies. It is a hands-on spirituality that demands dedication, but also offers great personal rewards.

Useful Sources

For further information on Celtic Reconstruction, you may want to check out these useful sources:

A Circle of Stones, by Erynn Rowan Laurie

Dictionary of Celtic Myth and Legend, by Miranda J. Green

Celtic Rituals: Guide to Ancient Celtic Spirituality, by Alexei Kondratiev

Hellenismos: Glory of Olympus

The culture of Greece and the beauty of its spirit have been reborn into the modern Pagan world. Greek civilisation may have changed, but the Gods of Olympus still come to those who call on them, bringing the Greek culture of old onto the international arena. The temples of the Gods are rebuilt, but stone columns have given way to pillars of spiritual devotion.

Old Temples to Neon Lights

Hellenismos is the religious path of the ancient Greek, faithfully reconstructed for Pagans in the modern world. Through this religion, followers seek to be true to adherence of the public and family ways of honouring the Gods, in a manner that is as close that of the ancient Greeks as is possible and appropriate. Hellenismos is sometimes referred to as Hellenic Reconstruction, which simply means that it is concerned with worshipping the Gods and Goddesses of the Hellenic Greeks in an authentic manner. "Hellenic" refers to a particular time in Greek history and is generally marked as beginning with the conquest of Alexander the Great. However, in practice, Hellenes (those who practice Hellenismos) base their spirituality on the time spanning from the Minoan Era, through the Hellenic Era and up to the Christianisation of Rome. But to give it a simple summary, Hellenics worship the Gods as they were in ancient Greece, before Christianity took hold.

The Minoan age takes this religious path all the way back to the seventh millennium BCE! But most Hellenes tend to focus primarily upon the time of classical and Hellenic Greece, which persisted from around the fourth Century BCE. All that being said, it must be pointed out that although Hellenes attempt to follow the path of the ancient Greeks, Hellenismos is nonetheless a modern religion and came into being around the early to mid 1990's, although many Pagans were already following the Greek Gods long before the proper founding of Hellenismos.

Hellenismos is a very diverse religious path and allows the follower to be equally diverse, just as the Greeks themselves were. The religion of the ancient Greeks had no formal doctrine regarding what was considered canon or the right way to serve a particular God. Instead, there existed a great deal of variety in forms of worship and belief across the Greek world and over the stretch of time. Different city states had different times for festivals and many had festivals that were entirely unique to their own city, the ways in which people celebrated their religion differed to various degrees from place to place and people held different views of the Gods and life, often influenced by great philosophers such as Plato, Socrates and Aristotle. In fact, the path of Hellenismos has a very close link to philosophy as studying the great philosophical writings of the time help us to uncover how the Greeks lived an how they viewed their world, including their perception of the divine. It should be pointed out, though, that this great diversity is not a license for the modern Hellenes to mix together whatever they want and call it Hellenismos. Indeed, the focus must be upon those things that are true to ancient Greek culture, as opposed to that of the Celts, the Jews, the Norse, etc. and modern religions and ideas such as Wicca and the New-Age movement.

Ways of Worship

Being as the methods of worship were so diverse amongst the ancient Greeks, how can we know the best ways to use? That is indeed a very good question. Methods of Hellenic worship can effectively be divided into these areas:

Prayers

These represent one of the most important aspects of Hellenic worship and have a place in the religion at all levels, both public and private. Prayer is has many different levels within Hellenismos. Primarily it is a means by which one may communicate directly with the Gods as an act of devotion to them, but it also a means to make respectful requests of the Gods or to simply share private aspects of your life with the Gods as a way to be closer to them. Prayers are used to mar the commencement of new things and to ask the blessings of the Gods in all new ventures. Most Hellenismos will seek to pray at the beginning of each new day, but will also be likely to pray elsewhere in the day where it feels appropriate. Which God or Goddess you pray to will depend greatly upon which has the greatest connection to the matter at hand, or possibly the one with the closest connection to the place that you are in. When in doubt, offer your prayers to Zeus. As chief among the Gods he has connections to many things and is grand over-seer.

The area in which Hellenic prayers will differ to many religions is in their structure, as Hellenic prayers tend to go by a set formula. Prayers are performed in a standing position with hands offered outwards. First you determine the whereabouts of the God you are petitioning. If they are a God connected with the sky or that act as overseers, then you raise your arms to the sky in veneration when praying. If the God is connected to water, then you extend your arms forward towards the water as if to embrace the God. If the God is a God of the Earth or the underworld, then extend your arms forwards again, but angled downwards slightly, as if you are offering your hands to the God.

Once you have assumed the appropriate stance then, with eyes wide and with a clear voice, you declare your prayer as follows:

Invitation: Call out to the God or Goddess of your choice and invite them into your presence so that they may hear your prayer. This should be accompanied a declaration of the God's greatness and their deeds.

Justification: At this point you must prove your own worthiness and explain to the God why they should hear your prayers. The point of this is not to boast or because the Greek deities are generally unwilling to help people, this is as sign of your own devotion to them by explaining the things you have done for the God out of love and respect for them. Greek society is based on reciprocation and so a person should prove that they are willing to serve others before they can expect anything in return.

Petition/Thanks: Once this is all done, you may commence your request of the deity or otherwise offer them thanks for the things that they have already done in your life.

The most important thing to remember when communicating with the Gods is to maintain reverence and respect for them. You are not giving them orders, you are inviting them in as special force in your life and requesting that they continue to be in your life in a good way. So when giving prayers it is right to speak true and from the heart, just as you would with your closest friends.

Hymns

In many ways, hymns are the same as prayers. They both seek to venerate the Gods and in some cases they are used to celebrate the Gods' great achievements, as well as how they have affected our own lives. The difference though, is that hymns are sung and may also be put to music. Given the musical nature of a hymn, they need not necessarily follow the proscribed method for crafting a prayer, but they should still contain the same amount of respect and reverence.

Offerings

In Hellenism the Gods are not distant and untouchable; they are very real forces in the lives of their followers. They are members of the greater society of the cosmos, of which humanity is just one rung and so they interact with humanity based upon the same societal guidelines that mankind holds in esteem. For the Greeks of old, their society was one based upon reciprocity, where society rewards those who contribute to it. In other words, you live up to your responsibilities in the world and help to make it a more pleasant place and then your are rewarded by sharing in those pleasantries, as everyone else should also be benefiting society in the same kind of way. This is the meaning of offering. The Gods are not given offerings as payment or a bribe to get them to help. Instead, offerings represent that we are willing to give back to the Gods as well, recognising that they are also part of our community and so deserve the same (or greater) level of reciprocation for all that they do.

Offerings come in two forms, sacrifices and votive offerings. Votive offerings represent the fulfilment of a vow made to the Gods, such as "Zeus, as you aid me through this, I shall gift you with seven baskets of the finest fruit of the Earth". In this way a votive gift would be given as the culmination of something, marking the fulfilment of what was offered, or as a gift. Sacrifices bring to mind ideas of killing animals and in larger rituals of old this did indeed occur, though today few Hellenismos have the resources for this kind of thing or otherwise see it as inappropriate these days. But a sacrifice need not be like this and the majority of the time will be a lot more humble. In fact, most Hellenes will perform sacrifices on a daily basis, gifting the Gods a cut of meat or/and a libation of wine. Indeed in Hellenic households it is common custom to offer the first drink of wine (poured into a bowl or the earth as a libation) to the Goddess Hestia, who is the Goddess of the hearth.

There is, however, another form of offering that one may devote to the Gods: that of deeds, acts and personal virtue.
With this, the person shows their devotion to the Gods by fulfilling all vows made to them and by living a good, productive and virtuous life that shows respect for the Gods and society. Making a vow and fulfilling it is actually a fairly common form of offering and considered to be quite significant, as it is not simply the giving of a gift, but the showing of devotion by actually living that devotion. It is also an example of your own virtue, which is important and examples you as fit for the attention and respect of the Gods.

Rituals
Rituals have many functions in Hellenismos and worship is one such function. There are many different kinds of rituals that you may wish to perform depending upon whether or not you are in a group and what historical examples you are basing it on. But modern Hellenes tend to perform rituals that follow this protocol:

Appropriate dress: A ritual is a big deal, especially when it is being used to offer worship to the Gods. Thus, it is appropriate to dress properly for it. This tends to mean the wearing of official white robes.
Procession: The procession is the journey to the point of the ritual. This can be as elaborate as a great parade in the streets, or a simple walk to the altar space. Often some in the procession will be bearing torches, while others carry any offerings that are to be given.

Purification: Whoever is acting as the leading priest or priestess will then purify themselves and those gathered, usually by splashing them with a mixture of water and sea-salt. The altar is then purified, either using the same salt water mix or, more commonly, by scattering barley grain over the altar.

Offerings: All offerings are then brought to the altar to be given to the Gods. This often commences with the first offering being given to Hestia. Once this and all other ritual activities are done, the remaining food and drink is shared among those gathered, with the first piece of food (especially if meat) being given to the God or Goddess of the ritual.

The Dodekatheon

The Gods of Hellenismos, called the Dodekatheon, otherwise known as the Olympian Gods, make up the central body of the Greeks Gods. In actuality the Greek Gods are incredibly numerous, many of them being the sons and daughters of other Gods, but the twelve Olympian Gods are the primary deities that most Hellenes regard.

Zeus: The chief and king of the Gods, renowned for wielding the mighty power of the thunderbolt. Zeus is the son of the Titans Rhea and Cronos, the latter of whom he overthrew after causing him to regurgitate all his sons and daughters (who were the other Gods), thus earning his place as ruler.

Hera: The wife of Zeus and queen of Olympus. She is best known for her jealous outbursts upon Zeus' various mistresses and their offspring. Hera is primarily concerned with the areas of marriage, women and fidelity.

Poseidon: The God of the oceans. He is often viewed as a tempestuous God that is easily angered, but this is also a reflection of his unwavering authority. Poseidon is primarily associated with the sea and rivers, horses and earthquakes.

Apollo: Apollo is a God of light, associated with the sun. He is seen as an archer, whose arrows are the flaming rays of the sun that never miss their target. He is primarily concerned with music, poetry, healing, prophecy and the arts.

Artemis: She is the virgin Goddess of the hunt who wanders in the wild places. Many associate her with the moon, which is fitting as she is the twin sister of Apollo, who is associated with the sun. Artemis is primarily concerned with animals, chastity, children and the protection of her sacred forest.

Athena: She is the Goddess of wisdom and the patron protector of the city of Athens, which still bears her name. She is regarded as a great warrior and extremely wise. Athena's primary concerns are education, the arts and war.

Ares: Ares is the God of War and the son f Zeus and Hera. As God of War, this is his primary centre of concern, but he also takes interest in issues of strength, martial prowess and in some cases, assertive lust and virility.

Hermes: Hermes is the messenger of the Gods and in this capacity is the God of Guidance, who watches over travellers of all varieties – both physically and spiritually. He is concerned with travel, trade and animal husbandry.

Aphrodite: The Goddess of Love. She is connected to love in all its forms, as well as beauty and sexuality. When Aphrodite was born she was the most beautiful of the Gods, so Zeus gave her in marriage to Hephaestus in order to stop the other Gods warring over here. However, she had many affairs. Her main concerns are love, the sea, beauty and sex.

Hephaestus: Hephaestus is the smith of the Gods, the God of Fire and the forge. He is the God that is closest to workmanship, especially the construction of weaponry. His chief concerns are the forge, construction, the mastery of fire, and crafts.

Dionysus: Centrally, Dionysus is the God of Wine and revelry, though in his Mystery Cults they may have explored many other associations to him. As it is, his primary concerns are wine, parties, drunkenness and sexuality.

Demeter: Demeter is the Goddess of Agriculture, who taught humanity how to work the land. She controls the fertility of the earth and the raising of crops.

In addition to these are Hades and Hestia. Hades is the God of the underworld, who took this area for his realm when the world was divided between him and his brothers, with Zeus ruling from the sky and Poseidon ruling the ocean. But Hades is still a very important God and holds a prominent place within the Greek pantheon. Hestia is the Goddess of the Hearth, who voluntarily gave up her place on Olympus so that she could dwell among humanity. Because of her care for mankind, she is afforded special favours in the homes of Hellenes, being given the libations before each meal and receiving prayers each day.

This is certainly not the limit of Greek deities that may be honoured, there are a great many more, such as Pan, Priapus and the Fates, to name but a few. There are also a great variety of other spiritual being to which Hellenes may offer certain honours and accords, such as Heroes and daemons. Heroes are those legendary figures of old whose deeds have made them particularly note worthy and have in some way ascended to a divine or semi-divine status, or have otherwise earned the right to such honours. Examples of these would be the great hero Achilles, wise Odysseus and Jason. Daemons, on the other hand, technically refers to any spiritual being (including Gods), but the word is often used to refer to those spiritual being that below the Gods, such as the spirits of places and things, but also various wandering spirits. The term may be used to commonly apply to things like nymphs and spirits both good and bad. The most highly regarded daemon is Agathos Daemon, who the "good spirit" of the household, commonly represented by the image of a snake. Agathos Daemon is the guardian of the house and so receives a special libation in its name, which is poured at the end of the main household meal.

Philosophy

The Greek view of the world in regards to religion rests more or less on the shoulders of the individual to determine. However, the religions of ancient Greece were strongly influenced by the cultural involvement of philosophers, such as Plato and Aristotle. These philosophies allow the individual to explore concepts like religion, society and the soul in a deep way and to find their own interpretation of them. Of course, the Hellene is under no demand to follow these philosophies, but a familiarity with them will at least provide the individual with a keen insight to the ancient Greek mind and the prominent ideas that influenced the development of their relationship with the Gods.

But with that being said, these philosophies do tend to espouse certain spiritual ideas that were important to Hellenic culture. Amongst these were the ideas of the soul and the afterlife. These are perhaps some of the most important concepts to deal with in Hellenismos and deserve a mention here.

The Soul

One of the chief beliefs in Hellenismos is in the existence of an eternal soul, which is the vital essence of each person. The philosopher Sallustius considered the body to be the vessel of the soul, through which it operates, yet the soul is not connected to the body. It is like a driver in a car, who begins life with no knowledge of how to drive. The soul must learn how to work the car and then how to navigate the road. In the same way, the soul must learn to find its way through life, by using a body that sometimes gets in the way or steers it in the wrong direction.

However, this does not *have* to be the view of the soul that you ascribe to. Indeed, different philosophers had different musings on the subject. But regardless, the existence of the soul is not only seen as a staple point of the religion, but also as a matter of logical sense to those involved.

The Afterlife

Greek religion primarily deals with the afterlife from three angles. The most common of these is that the dead descend into Hades to spend their afterlife as a Shade of their former self. There is also the view that the more deserving may spend their afterlives in The Asphodel Meadows, a place of natural beauty where the dead may dine upon Asphodel flowers.

To some though, the afterlife of Hades is simply a resting place for the soul before it drinks from the waters of forgetfulness and is reincarnated into a new life. Many within Hellenismos believe in reincarnation and again, it was a subject that was broached by many philosophers of the ancient world. Supposedly, a chosen few are able to avoid Hades all together and ascend to places of prominence amongst the Gods. The best example of this is the Hero Achilles, whose greatness was recognised by the Gods and so he was allowed to avoid a regular human death and marry in the afterlife. To some, Achilles even elevated to the position of a God in his own right.

An Overview

Hellenismos attempts not just to just to worship the Gods of Greece, but to also recapture the mentality and civility that the ancient Greeks enjoyed. It is more than a way to worship, it is also a way to look at the world and find your place within it, both philosophically and in physically. It teaches that we are accountable not only for ourselves, but also for the well-being of society and our fellow man. In Hellenismos, the Gods smile on those that accept their responsibilities and honour those who honour them.

Useful Sources

For further information on Hellenismos, you may want to check out these useful sources:

Hellenismos Today, by Timothy Jay Alexander

Greek Religion and Society, by Moses Finley

Old Stones, New Temples: Ancient Greek Paganism Reborn, by Drew Campbell

The Complete World of Greek Mythology, by R.G.A. Buxton

The Library of Greek Mythology, by Apollodorus

The Iliad, by Homer

The Odyssey, by Homer

The Aeneid, by Virgil

Shamanism: To Walk with the Spirit

Of all the Pagan paths Shamanism is perhaps all at once among the most diverse and misunderstood. Singers of tribal wisdom and movers among the unseen world, modern shamans have found a personal path of vision in solitude.

Roots and Branches

The roots of what we call Shamanism can be said to lay in the most ancient expressions of human religion and spirituality. The term 'Shaman' originally comes to us from the Tungus people who live in and around Siberia. To the Tungus, the "Šamán" is their holy man, who specialises in matters of magic and religion. The Tungus people are more commonly called the Evenki, today. The Evenki still practice their ancestral religion, though the term "Shamanism" has also come to refer to a wide variety of other religious practices that are similar to those of the Evenki. These are generally tribal-style practices that involve communication with and journeying to, the spirit world.

From these roots, modern Paganism can be said to have several varieties of Shamanism, all rather similar in their ethos, but perhaps different in their approach. Some modern Pagan Shamans hail from cultures with traditional shamanistic religions (such as those of South America) and have been initiated into these spiritual ways by other Shaman. These cultures may not use the words "Shaman" and "Shamanism" to describe themselves, but may be recognised as part of the larger family of traditional religions that are shamanistic in style. Other modern Pagans have specifically sought out training in the ways of traditional shamanistic religion, sometimes spending many years training under a religious leader of one of these cultures. However, for the majority of modern Pagans who recognise themselves as Shamans, the path is one of solitary discovery, as they seek to build or reconstruct a shamanic practice through a combination of studying world Shamanism and experiencing the world of the Shaman directly.

The Shaman Way

Shamans may utilise a variety of different practices, including, magic, healing, divination and meditation, but the central elements of Shamanism are most certainly ecstasy and communing with the spirit world. Shamanism is an animistic religion, which means that one of its primary beliefs is that the universe has a spiritual aspect and that it is populated by a variety of human and non-human spirits. The spiritual aspect of our world is closely interwoven with that of the physical and all things can be said to have a spiritual dimension to them. Very often this means that even things like trees, rocks, rivers and animals have their own spirits, which the Shaman may come to know. But the Shaman may also come to know other spirits who embody larger concepts, such as tribal spirits and totem spirits.

Ecstasy is the means by which a Shaman may commune with the spirit world and even journey into it. Ecstasy means that Shaman use techniques like dance and rhythmic drumming in order to enter into a trance. While in this trance state, the Shaman is able to see and speak with spirits, and is likely to go on journeys into the spirit realm itself, leaving behind their physical form.

The tools of Shamanism may vary from place to place and from person to person, especially depending upon which culture a Shaman draws from to craft their practices. Some modern Shamans may base their practices in ancient Celtic ideas, others in South American tribalism, others in African tribal practices, or perhaps the practices of North American religions, such as those of the Inuit people. There is also a wealth of shamanistic traditions spanning across Asia, as well as certain elements of the aboriginal religions of Australia. With modern technology, information on all of these traditions are now accessible to modern Pagans in a way that they have ever been before and an aspiring Shaman can look into them all and (re)construct their spiritual path by drawing from the shamanic tradition that they feel most connected to, or perhaps creating a unique practice that draws from many different world traditions.
However, that being said, there are certain things are often utilised by modern Shamans.

Drumming: The drum is a common tool of the modern Shaman, referred to by some as "the Shaman's horse". Through drumming, one is able to achieve the ecstatic state needed to journey into the spirit world. By beating a drum in regular, rhythmical strokes, the Shaman causes a transformation in the mind of the listener. In scientific terms, the drumming causes a change in the person's brain waves and allows them to enter an altered state of consciousness.

Dancing: Ecstatic dance has been used in many cultures as a means for achieving altered states of consciousness. This type of dancing has a similar effect to that of drumming, where through a combination of excited movement, accelerated breathing and music, a change in brain waves is brought about and thus brings the Shaman into an altered state of consciousness.

Chanting: Chanting and singing, is another way to enter into a trance state and has been used by many world religions and cultures. The Vedic (ancient Indian) religions, for example, use chanted Mantras as a means of meditation, by which the conscious state is changed.There are many different kinds of chanting, such as chanting names, phrases, songs, a holy word, or even just the intoning of certain sounds, whose resonance aids the change in consciousness.

These three methods may be used individually, but are often combined in order to produce the optimum effect in changing consciousness.

While drumming, dancing and chanting are among the most common tools of Shamanism, they are by no means the entirety of what Shamans use. For example, Shamans have a close connection to the natural world and among Shamans of indigenous tribes, a Shaman may have knowledge of local plants which may be used to aid in altering ones consciousness for the purpose of journeying into the spirit world. However, it must be noted that these Shaman are trained and experienced in their local herb lore and you should never try using plants in this way, if you have not had professional training. Doing so can put your health at risk. For those of us who do not have access to that kind of training and can't afford to buy a drum, there are alternatives that the modern Pagan can substitute. In the simplest sense, anything from a washing up bowl to a rubbish bin, can be used as a make-shift drum. Alternatively, there are many shamanism CD's and downloads now on the market, with pre-recorded drumming, designed to offer the listener a variety of different journeying experiences. For those wishing to save a little money, there are also a lot of videos of pre-recorded shamanic drumming available on the internet, through sites like Youtube.

Healer and Holy Man

While it is often the way of the Shaman to walk alone, there are also aspects of Shamanism that connect to the community and the world in general. The Shaman can be said to work on three sides of the human experience, learning skills in the physical, mental and spiritual. The physical sense, indigenous shaman often have knowledge about the healing properties of plants and other medicinal methods for curing the body of ailments. In the mental sense, the Shaman is often like a therapist, using traditional shamanic methods of ritual and journeying to bring healing to those who are psychologically suffering. Then, of course, the Shaman must also play a role in the spiritual side of life, often healing or rebuilding the spirit of those who need it, or escorting lost souls and spirits to where they should be.

Remember, the Shaman is a specialist in these things. In indigenous shamanistic cultures, the people are well aware of the reality of the spirit world around them and that their lives may be influenced by it, but when they require help or healing, be it physical, mental or spiritual, they go to the Shaman, because he is the one trained in those ways. The Shaman learns the herbs that heal the body. He learns how to lead people in journeys so that they can be healed and he journeys himself, for the good of those who need it. Of course, many modern Pagans who follow the path of Shamanism, may rarely find themselves approached by someone needing mental or spiritual healing, and of course, those needing physical healing should refer to a doctor before trying any alternative therapies. But there are those who do offer these kinds of Shamanic services. Either way, these are important skills for a Shaman and they take time to learn, either under the tutelage of another Shaman or through direct instruction from the spirits.

Working with the Spirit

It is not unusual for a Shaman to develop relationships with specific spirits, such as gaining a spirit guide, who aids them in personal development and tasks, or a power animal, which acts as a guardian and protector for the Shaman. The Shaman may also seek out particular spirits in order to gain their aid or wisdom, as it is commonly recognised that certain spirits possess wisdom and expertise in particular areas. For example, many regard the spirit of Crow to be an invaluable companion in navigating the underworld, while others recognise the spirit of Coyote to be a cunning master of riddles and trickery. Other spirits may be sought for help in healing, answering questions, learning life skills, empowerment and any other areas where the Shaman may require aid.

But the journey of the Shaman isn't necessarily just an external one, going forth into the spirit world. The Shaman's journey is often also an internal one, exploring their own spirit and psyche, in order to better understand themselves, enact change in their lives and who they are, and also to heal themselves of those emotional and spiritual scars that life has given them. Indeed, personal development and experience, is very important in Shamanism, as it is through experience of the spirit, both within and without, that the Shaman gains understanding of the world and their position within it.

One way in which a Shaman may achieve this kind of development and greater personal understanding, is though *shape-shifting*. Shamanic shape-shifting is not literally the transformation of ones body into something else, such as turning into a jaguar. Instead, shamanic shape-shifting is primarily a spiritual and mental transformation, in which the Shaman learns to metamorphose into another form, granting them understanding of that form and access to the advantages of their new form. Though, it is often the case, that while undergoing this kind of shape-shifting experience, the Shaman's body will in some ways also come to resemble ad move like that which they are seeking to transform into; especially if they are using a medium like ecstatic dance to enter the required trance state.

So, in this way, a Shaman would undergo a *spiritual* transformation into a jaguar (etc.), while they are journeying in the spirit world, in order to better commune with that spirit, understand them and learn from them.

One becomes what it is they wish to know.

The Otherworlds

One may ask 'what is the spirit world of the Shaman?', 'where is this place to which they go and what things do they see?'

The Otherworlds are pure experience made manifest, where mind and body become redefined. It is a place populated by spirits and where folk tale and myth become the signposts of truth. It is a journey in which we hang ourselves upon the tree of the world and learn to speak in the language of visions. As one might imagine, placing the Shaman's world of the spirit into words, is not an easy task. It is a complex geography of thought and form. Many Shaman recognise the Otherworld to be divided into three parts: The Upper World, The Middle World and The Lower World. It may be useful to imagine these "worlds" as parts of a tree, with the branches being the Upper World, reaching into the heavens and existing among the stars and the astral bodies, the trunk is the Middle World of earthly things, and the roots of the tree are the Lower World, descending into the hidden depths, where in darkness the roots find nourishment to live.

The Upper World: The Shaman may rise up through the clouds and enter into The Upper World, often undergoing a powerful (and sometimes painful) transformation or rebirth in order to access this place. On the new-grown wings, the reborn Shaman may ascend to this place and meet with teachers, ancestors and celestial beings.

The Middle World: In The Middle World, the Shaman may meet with guides who help him in gaining knowledge and understanding pertaining to our physical world. Uncovering what is lost, discovering solutions in life or journeying across the globe, the Shaman navigates within the spiritual reflection of the physical plane. For some, this may be similar to what others describe as Out of Body Experiences.

The Lower World: A Shaman will often journey to The Lower World in order to seek a power animal or spirit guide, with whom they can connect. As with all other areas of the Otherworlds, The Lower World is a complex geography and is often seen to be the dwelling place for the dead, or perhaps it is better to say the dead who are preparing for rebirth.

It is important not to think of the different "worlds" in terms of positive or negative. For instance, The Upper World is not heaven and The Lower World is not Hell. As much as The Lower World may often appear dark and play host to the dead, it can also be a place of life, light and discovery. Similarly, The Upper World may appear to be "in the heavens", but one should not expect to be greeted by a host of angels who are all to happy to show you paradise. Each part of the Otherworld has diversity and there are spirit beings that are willing to help you and there are spirit beings that are not. Just like going anyway, there are places where a person will be more welcome, places that better destinations for specific purposes and places that the inexperienced traveler should not go. That is why the Shaman must be a master of their experiences.

While journeying into the Otherworlds is a important part of Shamanism, it is not to be taken lightly. The Shaman goes to the Otherworld with a specific purpose. It's not a holiday destination or somewhere to play. The spirit world should be treated with respect and so should those beings who live there. But in the Shaman philosophy, the same applies to our physical world. Both are intrinsically intertwined and one must respect nature and its power, on both sides of the veil.

But perhaps the most important thing to remember about the Shamanic spiritual view, is that we exist within a world that is living in every regard and that is populated by a great tapestry of spirits, who embody and reflect the living world, right down to the rocks, trees and the land itself. The Shaman connects with both sides of the world, walking in the spiritual and physical realms. An explorer, an ambassador, a healer, a warrior, a student, a teacher.

An Overview

Shamanism is perhaps the foundation of all religion. At the very least most, if not all, Pagan religions have shamanistic elements in their heritage. To be a Shaman is to live in two worlds at once, with an eye to the spirit and an eye to the physical – walking on both sides of the veil. The Shaman is a healer and a guide, often working alone, but also there for the community when needed. Through his skills, he brings about transformation within and becomes one with the world without.

Useful Sources

For further information on Shamanism, you may want to check out these useful sources:

Shamanism (Piatkus Guides), by Gordon MacLellan

Singing the Soul Back Home: Shamanism in Daily Life, by Caitlin Matthews

Shamanic Experience: A Practical Guide to Contemporary Shamanism, by Kenneth Meadows

Shamans: Siberian Spirituality and the Western Imagination, by Ronald Hutton

Kemeticism: Path of the Black Land

The Kemetic path revives the traditional spirituality of Egypt, bringing into the modern world, the practices and faith connected to some of the oldest expressions of divinity in the world. Finding it's heritage in this ancient civilisation, Kemeticism draws upon many thousands of years of divine revelation and religious practice, recorded upon papyrus and carved into the walls of some of the world's greatest ancient monuments.

Ways of the Black Land

Kemet, a word from the ancient Egyptians themselves, used to describe their own land. It means "black land" or "black soil", referring to the rich, black soil that would be deposited by the River Nile, that was the source of agricultural life for the people of this country. The Nile and its black soil was the source of life and could be said to be the foundation upon which ancient Egyptian culture was built. It is this culture that Kemeticism seeks to capture and revive – specifically, the spiritual philosophies and practices of ancient Egypt. While there are many Pagans who find inspiration in Egyptian spirituality and a connection to the Gods of Egypt, Kemeticism is a reconstructionist religion, meaning that it specifically tries to utilise practices and ideas that are as close to those of the ancient Egyptians themselves, as one can be in the modern day, rather than seeking to know Egyptian Gods, magic, etc. through more modern Pagan systems. Because of this, Kemeticism, like other reconstructionist religions, places a high value on historical research and archeology, to help practitioners discover the historical details of Kemetic faith.

Kemeticism is primarily a polytheistic faith, meaning that followers of this religion believe in many Gods and Goddesses. Though, there are also variations in this belief. For example, some Kemetics would describe themselves as monotheists, believing in a single divine being, who manifests in many forms. These Gods would be worshiped in temple cults, at festivals and in the homes of the people. However, modern Paganism is rather smaller and Pagans of each faith are often spread out over great distances, and so modern Kemeticism is arguably practiced primarily in the home, as there is currently limited organisation and numbers in a single region for practitioners to form cults and celebrate festivals together, let alone raise temples to be new houses of the Gods, tended by a modern priesthood, as was the case in ancient times. Though, Internet groups and websites do allow for some degree of community among Kemetics and priesthood have been set up, usually operating on a more long-distance basis. One such example is the Kemetic Orthodoxy, who train and appoint clergy into a priesthood modeled upon those of ancient Egypt.

Neteru

The Gods and Goddesses of Kemeticism are collectively known as Neteru (singularly Neter). Neteru roughly translates as deities or "powers of nature". There are arguably several thousand Neteru in Kemetic religion and so it would be impossible to discuss them all here. However, the following Gods are the most widely known and revered, both in modern Kemetic religion and its ancient equivalent.

Ra: Falcon-headed Ra, God of solar light and triumph, is the father of the Neteru and of mankind. He is recognised in a variety of forms, but is best known as the boatman of the sun, who rises each day in the east, guides the sun across the sky and then departs into the west, where he descends into the underworld, to triumphantly return to the living world at the next sunrise.

Aset: Better known to most, under her Greek name of Isis, Aset is a Goddess of life, magic and wisdom. She is the divine mother, whose protective wings have spread wide across the world, making her one of the most widely regarded Goddesses of both the ancient and modern world. The Romans carried her worship all the way to Britain, where they built a temple to her in the city that is now London. While modern Pagans across the globe revere her in a way that is unparalleled. She is best known as the life giving Goddess who searched the world to collect and reassemble the pieces of her husband's body, allowing her to then give birth to the great God, Heru.

Ausur: Again, better known under his Greek name of Osiris. He is the husband and brother of Aset. Ausur sits in the netherworld, the finest of rulers, who judges the dead. But he is also the bringing of abundance, as he draws in the black, rich Nile soil that makes farming possible. His most famous myth is that of his death at the hands of his brother, Set, whereby he entered the netherworld to assume his new throne.

Heru: Also known as Horus, the God Heru is a king, a warrior and the sky-ruling overseer, whose eyes are the sun and moon. Represented by a hawk, he is the maker of pharaohs. Like the hawk, he swoops cunningly upon his opponents and uses his skill and wiles to protect mankind and the land of Kemet. Because of this, the right of rulership is his to give. Heru is the avenger. Born of the Goddess Aset, he brings justice upon Set for the murder of his father, Ausur and so wins the throne of the land.

Set: Set is the necessary chaos of the universe. He is the destroyer, existing as a force of nature and like a force of nature he is beyond concepts of good and evil. A ravaging sand-storm or the power of a wild bull. He embodies the virility of raw masculinity. Set is the slayer of Ausur, but in so doing he also defines the role of Heru and gifts the underworld with its king.

Ma'at: Ma'at is more than a Goddess, she is a central force to strive after, deserving of its own section of separate discussion. She is the purest light of Ra. His daughter, bringing balance to the universe, the essential way of all things that maintains creation. She is justice, balance, order and righteousness. Her way is the true way. The principle of truth that unifies all things.

Anpu: You will recognise this Neter as the black jackal/dog headed God, whom the Greeks named Anubis. He is a psychopomp, which means he guides the dead from the land of the living, into the netherworld. In this role he oversees the funeral rites of those who have died and then accompanies them to the hall of Double Ma'at, where their heart is weighed against a feather of Ma'at, to judge the worthiness of the soul in the afterlife.
Anpu is a guide and guardian for the dead, escorting them to where they belong, silently comforting them on their journey to the next world.

Het-Hert: The Neter Het-Hert is the embodiment of the perfect mother. Depicted as the divine cow, she is seen to be a patient, caring provider, whose four legs stand at the four corners of creation. As the cow suckles her calf, Het-Hert likewise provides for creation. Depicted as a woman with cows horns holding the disc of the sun, she is not merely a mother Goddess, but the absolute quintessential mother, flowing with love.

Ptah: Ptah is the great unknowable source of all. The master craftsman and creator, who brought forth all things from himself. Some may compare him to the more abstract ideas of the Judeo-Christian God, as a great creator who is beyond human comprehension, yet is a divine king to be praised.

As a craftsman, he is closely connected to human crafts and labours of creation.

Bast: One of the most popular of the Neteru among modern Pagans, she is depicted as a cat or cat-headed woman. She is the one who dances forth nimbly from creation, traversing all places. In her earliest incarnations, she is like the lion, ferocious; the one who tears apart. But she is also like the domestic cat, a love of pleasure, joy and sexuality. In many ways, she is also a walker in two worlds, making her home in the sun and holding the light of the moon in her eyes by night. She is magical and surrounded by mystery.

Sekhmet: Where Bast has her ferocious aspect, tempered by joy and pleasure, Sekhmet mirrors her with the pure violent fury of an avenging huntress. She is the vengeful hand of Ra, depicted as a lioness, who punishes those who deserve it. She is the righter of wrongs, protecting and avenging the innocent, with savage abandon.

The most famous myth of Sekhmet sees her sent forth by Ra to reign in the lawless and unrighteous behaviour of mankind. An army is sent against her, which she defeats and provides them the chance to withdraw, but when they do not, she becomes enraged and begins to slaughter them indiscriminately. Ra realises that Sekhmet must be made to stop her savage assault, before mankind is destroyed and so he instructs her handmaidens to create a lake of beer and mandrake. When Sekhmet comes across it, she believes it to be blood, which in her savage rage, she drinks. The drink causes her to fall asleep and her rage passes.

Tehuti: More commonly known by his Greek name of Thoth, Tehuti is a God of wisdom and knowledge. He is the divine scribe and creator of writing, making him all at once a God of learning and communication. As the divine scribe, he records all things, all that has ever happened and all deeds performed by each person. He has knowledge of all things, all places and all time and is thus also the master of time itself. With his unparalleled knowledge and wisdom, he accompanies Ma'at, for he knows not only how all things are, but also how all things must be. Tehuti is the wisest of judges and keeper of all knowledge.

Daily Ritual

Ritual and worship in ancient Egypt existed in two forms; the state religion, with its large festivals and temple based worship, and household religion which was the concern of the individual and the family. This second form of Kemetic religion is best focused on here, so that you're better able to begin taking part in Kemeticism yourself.

Because household worship was private to the family or individual, little information has survived regarding the structure of this form of worship, though it is generally accepted that a household would have it's own altar or shrine, most likely dedicated to a Neter that is important to the family or individual that lives there. However, even though there is little historical information on these practice, it is possible for the modern practitioner to take what we know of the state religion and adapt it to home worship, as it is very likely that certain practices and concepts of worship were common at all levels of Egyptian society.

In its form, Kemetic daily rituals were rather similar to those performed by modern Hindus, focusing upon the attendance of a sacred shrine and statue. Firstly, a servant of the Neter would perform a purification upon oneself and the area in which the shrine is located, using water and incense to cleanse the area. Of course, for modern practitioners, it is probably rare that you'll be able to allocate a room of your house especially for a shrine. But, as many modern Pagans do, you can place an altar or shrine somewhere in your house, such as your bedroom or living room. You can then use incense around the altar space in order to cleanse it and prepare it for your daily rituals. In ancient Egypt, a substance known as Natron was commonly used in the purification of shrines. Natron is a substance that is naturally occurring in Egypt and modern practitioners are unlikely to be able to get their hands on any. However, if you truly feel the need, you may be able to "make" your own artificial Natron, by mixing sodium bicarbonate (baking soda) and sodium carbonate (washing soda) in a roughly 50/50 ratio, with a few pinches of table salt. Natron is like an early form of soap, with many varied uses for the body and household. If you wish to use it in the cleansing of yourself and your shrine, feel free, though many modern practitioners are happy using modern soap products.

Once the shrine area has been cleansed, the faithful servant kneels before the shrine and offers prayers and invocations to the deity that the shrine houses. The statue of the Neter is then brought forward, clothed, given jewelery and is "fed" offerings, such as milk and water, and food may also be left at the shrine as a daily offering.

This ritual is in many cases repeated in the evening, though generally without the feeding of the deity. In this way the deity, through their shrine and statue, is treated like an honored guest in the home or even a member of the family.

Here are some examples of prayers and recitations used in ancient Egypt, as part of daily temple worship. You may wish to use these as they appear here, or perhaps instead you could use these examples as a guide for how you can structure prayers and recitations of your own.

> Awaken! Be at peace!
> May you awaken in peace:
> Awaken O Amen-Re, lord of the thrones of the two lands, in peace!

The above is a morning prayer from the Karnak Temple ritual. This morning prayer was said as the priest entered the sanctuary.

> Be pure, O Amun!
> Receive your bread,
> Receive your incense,
> Receive your divine offerings which are the eye of Heru!

Papyrus Chester Beatty 9

The Egyptians did not believe that the statues themselves were divine, nor did they worship the statues. Instead, the statues and images used in rituals, provided a focus though which human offerings and devotion could be channeled to the divine. Though, a statue had to be made ready for this kind of use, through rituals of purification that made the statue ready to be used as a channel to the Gods. This ritual was know as *The Opening of The Mouth*. This same ritual was also performed upon the dead, in order to allow them to awaken and gain their senses and breath in the afterlife.

The Opening of the Mouth ceremony made the statue a suitable vehicle for channeling the worship of the Gods and for allowing the divine to manifest through or within the statue. Again, this is very similar to modern Hinduism.

The Opening of the Mouth

In order for you to perform the Opening of the Mouth ceremony, a simplified version is provided here, so that you can make your statue(s) ready for use in your religious workings.

Before you begin, there are some things that you will need to do Firstly, you must cleanse your statue. Do so physically, making sure it is clean, and also using incense.

You will also need a ritual blade to perform this ritual. The ancient Egyptians used special ritual blades to perform the Opening of the Mouth, but it is unlikely that you will be able to find these, so you may wish to use a special ritual blade bought specifically for this ritual. Many Pagan shops will sell ritual blades, but of course, take care when using one. Your ritual blade should also be cleansed.

The Ritual

1. First, it is typical to call upon a deity (usually Heru) to grant you the power and right to perform the ritual.

2. Touch the tip of your blade upon the mouth of your statue, as if you are going to cut open the mouth.

3. Say the following:

> O Netjer, I have come in search of thee; I am Horus.
> I have pressed for thee thy mouth. I am thy son, thy beloved. I have opened for thee thy mouth.
> I have adjusted for thee thy mouth to thy bones!
> I open for thee thy mouth; I open for thee thine eyes, O Netjer.
> I open for thee thy mouth with my blade of copper (or, iron), which opens the mouth of the gods.
> Horus opens the mouth of this Netjer.
> With that wherewith he opened the mouth of his father; with that wherewith he opened the mouth of Osiris; with the copper, (or, iron) which comes forth from Set, the mśḫtiw-hook of
> copper (or, iron), which opens the mouth of the gods.

(The above words are an adaptation of the words of the Opening of the Mouth ritual, as found in the ancient Egyptian Pyramid Texts, Utterances 20-21)

4. As you do this, allow the blade to also touch the eyes, ears, hands and feet of the statue, also.
5. Once this is done, offerings can them be made to your statue.

With the ceremony performed, your statue may now be used for regular worship.

Ma'at

When discussing Kemetic religion, special mention must be given to Ma'at. Ma'at is a Goddess, but much more than this, Ma'at is the foundation of Egyptian society, religion and even the concept by which all things may know their place in the world.

Ma'at is the balance in all things and the struggle to maintain that balance. It is right order, right action, natural harmony, justice, truth and the way things must flow in order to maintain. It is the also the result of following the path of Ma'at. By adhering to Ma'at, one follows a path in which being true, just and at harmony with ones world, bring the equal reward of receiving truth, justice and harmony in ones life. Upholding Ma'at is the charge of all beings, including Gods and humans, and so all beings must seek to work together in order to maintain Ma'at. To uphold Ma'at is to be at one with Ma'at, living in the right order of nature and the right order of society, acknowledging that all things have their place and all mankind has a responsibility to contribute to the smooth and just running of their own society, by being true and responsible towards nature and their fellow man.

So Ma'at is not so much a moral code, but instead a natural law, by which one must be moral and responsible. It does not require a list of "thou shalt not's" in order to appease the will of a deity and thus be considered "good", instead it requires that a person be good in order to be at one with the natural harmony of the universe. Doing this makes a person part of Ma'at, not merely a follower of laws and rules. The harmony of Ma'at is it's own reward.

An Overview

The Kemetic path is one in which one seeks piety towards the Gods, with whom one seeks to achieve the balance of Ma'at and thus play a part in bringing about truth, justice and harmony on all levels of the universe. The Gods are like parents to us, able to comfort, teach and guide, but they also require us to play our part in the grand scheme and show dedication to that path. If we do so, then the Gods can be real forces in our lives and our homes, and all of life can be a celebration of truth, justice and order, through which all things become sacred.

Useful Sources

For further information on Kemeticism, you may want to check out these useful sources:

The Neteru of Kemet: An Introduction, by Tamara Siuda-Legan

Following the Sun : A Practical Guide to Egyptian Religion, by Sharon LaBorde

A Dictionary of Egyptian Gods and Goddesses, by George Hart

The Complete Gods and Goddesses of Ancient Egypt, by Richard H. Wilkinson

The Ancient Egyptian Prayerbook, by Tamara Siuda-Legan

Kemetic Orthodoxy - www.kemet.org

Eclectic Paganism – Ancient Approach, Modern Spirit

Modern Paganism is a religious movement of great variety, in which individuals may embrace what they find spiritually best for them, from among hundreds of religions and traditions from around the world and across human history. Eclectic Paganism represents an undefined middle road in which the modern Pagan has the freedom to build their own path, using all of these sources as inspiration.

The Pagan Umbrella

We live in an interesting time, where Paganism is moving and developing in ways that it never has done before and more and more people are finding that Paganism provides them with a freedom to express their spirituality, without boundaries and on their own terms. Though there are many different religions under the Pagan umbrella, the modern Pagan is not restricted to simply having to choose one and follow it. Indeed, we live in a time when Paganism itself can be a person's religion, rather than any specific Pagan religion, like Heathenry or Druidry. It's even fair to say that this form of Paganism without defined edges, is probably the largest and most popular form of modern Paganism. Many refer to this as Eclectic Paganism, as it tends to be unique to each individual and comprised of elements from a variety of different Pagan path. In some cases, an eclectic Pagan may even feel moved to aspects of other world religions that are often not thought of as being part of the modern Pagan movement.

But what does it really mean to be an Eclectic Pagan? Well, that is a question that only you can answer, should you decide to tread this free-form path. Eclectic Paganism is practiced differently by each such Pagan and everyone following this path will draw from different sources, guided by what feels spiritually *right* for them. That is why the details of Eclectic Paganism are ultimately only something that you can answer, because you are the only one who can decide what is right for you.

Eclecticism + Paganism

To be eclectic means that you derive your ideas, style, beliefs and practices, from a wide variety of sources. So to be an Eclectic Pagan means that you do this within the bounds of Paganism and its many different ideas, style, beliefs and practices.

Many Pagans will begin their Pagan faith on an eclectic path, as they first start to explore the many threads of Paganism. Over time, you will develop a greater sense of what sits right with you and how it all fits together. This may manifest as stepping onto the path of a more defined Pagan religion, such as Wicca, Shamanism or Druidry, or you may instead remain on an eclectic path and develop your own structure and practices to allow you to define your spirituality for yourself. But the final shape your spirituality takes is entirely in your hands. But then again, a large number of Pagans (eclectic and otherwise) find that their path never really takes on a "final shape" and instead continues to change and restructure over the years, as they learn more and have different experiences in their spiritual lives.

An Ancient Heritage

Eclecticism is often viewed as a form of spirituality without roots and for this reason some may see it as somehow less "genuine" than some of the other Pagan religions. But in reality, this isn't really the case. It's also not really right to say that Eclecticism doesn't have roots. In fact, by it's very nature, it has lots of different roots and is fed from a wide array of branches, as well. So in this sense, far from having no roots, Eclecticism is instead more like a tangled thicket of ideas. A hedgerow of spirituality.

But one can also say that Eclecticism has very distinct roots, or more specifically, that the practice of Eclecticism has a very ancient heritage. Eclecticism was a particular approach to philosophy in the ancient world, in which many ancient philosophers would determine their own philosophic view, drawn from the ideas of many different philosophers. This was particularly true among many of the philosophers of ancient Alexandria. In this ancient form of Eclecticism, philosophers were seeking to understand the natural world by drawing on a combination of the ideas of philosophy, religion and those ideas that would eventually become the foundations of science. Today, our knowledge of the natural world has progressed and modern Eclectic Pagans may well shape their view of the world, physically and spiritually, using their own selection of ideas from religion, philosophy and science. But of course, the sources you draw from, are entirely your choice and as has already been said, only you can determine what is right for you.

An Overview

Eclectic Paganism is a path that you have to craft yourself, drawing from the full range of the Pagan world, old and new, using your own spiritual judgment to discern what is most applicable to you and then putting it together into a system that works for you. Because ultimately these are the kinds of questions that every Pagan must ask themselves: What feels right to me? What works for me? And also, what doesn't work for me? The essence of Eclectic Paganism is the acknowledgment that there are many paths to spiritual fulfillment and no path is right or wrong – only right or wrong for you.

Pagan Generation

Know Thyself

This book is an introduction Pagan religion, presenting you with it's most popular paths and concepts. But modern Paganism is constantly growing, developing and transforming. It gains new branches, new members, new concepts and also recovers the ancient ways. Perhaps reading this book has given you an idea as to where you'd like to explore next. Perhaps you have a feeling growing inside you that is drawing towards a certain path or deity. If so, trust that feeling.

Paganism has come so far in just the past 100 years and the lessons that our elders have learnt are important and worthy of respect. But **YOU** are the future of Paganism. Now is your time. Those who have gone before you have carved out modern Paganism and brought it to life. Now that life is yours to live. You have the world at your fingertips. All those tools of the past are yours to use as you will, as you go boldly into the new dawn.

Your journey has begun. Now you must decide which path to take.

None can walk this path for you, for it is a journey that leads within.

Carved into the temple of Delphi are these words to the traveler: *Know thyself.*

> This above all: to thine own self be true,
> And it must follow, as the night the day,
> Thou canst not then be false to any man.
> - Shakespeare, Hamlet

Pagan Generation

www.ingramcontent.com/pod-product-compliance
Lightning Source LLC
Chambersburg PA
CBHW062218080426
42734CB00010B/1935